INTERRUPTED SEASONS

AND

THE UNSTOPPABLE GRACE OF GOD

FAMILY DEVOTIONS

May the Word of God be a
blessing to all who read it

Dave Nelson

BY REV. DAVID J. NELSON

Interrupted Seasons
Trilogy Christian Publishers A Wholly Owned Subsidary of Trinity
Broadcasting Network
2442 Michelle Drive Tustin, CA 92780

Rights Department, 2442 Michelle Drive, Tustin, CA 92780.
Trilogy Christian Publishing/TBN and colophon are trademarks of
Trinity Broadcasting Network.
Cover design by: Natalee Dunning
For information about special discounts for bulk purchases, please contact
Trilogy Christian Publishing.
Trilogy Disclaimer: The views and content expressed in this book are
those of the author and may not necessarily reflect the views and doctrine
of Trilogy Christian Publishing or the Trinity Broadcasting Network.
Manufactured in the United States of America
10 9 8 7 6 5 4 3 2 1
Library of Congress Cataloging-in-Publication Data is available.
ISBN: 978-1-63769-292-9
E-ISBN: 978-1-63769-293-6

ACKNOWLEDGEMENTS

I would like to thank my good friend, Rev. Dr. Daniel Schroeder, for all the help he gave me on my devotional book. Sandy and I have known Dan for over thirty years. He has been an encouragement to both of us. His assistance in compiling and editing *Interrupted Seasons* was very much appreciated.

I would like to take this opportunity to thank my dear wife, Sandy, who for fifty-four years has helped, encouraged, and supported me in all my endeavors. Her imagination, suggestions, and insight helped make *Interrupted Seasons* a book truly meant for such a time as this. She has been a blessing to my life and an asset to my ministry.

TABLE OF CONTENTS

Introduction - 1

Devotion 1
Interrupted - 3
James 1:16-17

Devotion 2
Invisible Enemies - 6
1 Peter 1:8-9

Devotion 3
Crack It Open - 9
Romans 11:33

Devotion 4
Only $19.95 - 12
Ephesians 2:8-9

Devotion 5
Teach Them About Jesus - 15
2 Timothy 1:3-5

Devotion 6
A Very Special Garden - 18
Matthew 26:36-38

Devotion 7
Secret Sins - 21
Romans 3:23-24

Devotion 8
Different, But Yet The Same - 24
Galatians 3:26-29

Devotion 9
Be Careful What You Say - 27
Ephesians 4:29-32

Devotion 10
Pretty Inside - 30
1 Corinthians 13:5-7a

Devotion 11
He Slept Too - 33
Romans 1:2-6

Devotion 12
What's A Penny Worth? - 36
Proverbs 3:1-6

Devotion 13
Who's Child Are You? - 39
Romans 8:14-18

Devotion 14
Pass It On - 42
2 Corinthians 5:17-21

Devotion 15
Rainbow - 45
Lamentations 3:22b-26

Devotion 16
Flipping Pancakes - 48
1 Corinthians 15:57-58

Devotion 17
Mosquitoes And Weeds - 51
Romans 7:19, 24-25a

Devotion 18
Camping Out With God - 54
1 John 4:9-11

Devotion 19
Thankful To Whom - 57
Philippians 4:6

Devotion 20
Why Did He Say No? - 60
1 John 5:11-15

Devotion 21
Packing Up - 63
2 Timothy 1:7

Devotion 22
Can You See The Light? - 66
2 Corinthians 4:3-5

Devotion 23
Which Cross? - 69
1 Corinthians 1:18

Devotion 24
Thank God For The Little Things - 71

Devotion 25
Covid-19 Tree - 74
1 Corinthians 4:1-2

Devotion 26
Which Is More Important? - 76
Philippians 2:5-8

Devotion 27
They Didn't Do A Thing - 79
Romans 12:21

Devotion 28
Buttered Bread - 82
James 3:8-10

Devotion 29
Why? - 85
Acts 4:12

Devotion 30
Are They Rich Or Poor? - 87
John 17:3

Devotion 31
What If? - 89
Philippians 4:6-7

Devotion 32
Signs Of God's Love - 91
Matthew 5:45

Devotion 33
To Miss The Target - 94
Titus 2:11-14

Devotion 34
Homeless - 97
Romans 8:28

Devotion 35
Seasons - 99
Ecclesiastes 3:1-5

Devotion 36
The Card - 102
Romans 8:17-18

Devotion 37
He Never Changes - 105
1 John 5:20

Devotion 38
Answer - 107
1 Peter 3:15

Devotion 39
Non-Essential Church - 109
2 Timothy 4:2-5

Devotion 40
Scrapbook - 112
James 1:17-19

Afterword - 115
About The Author - 117

INTRODUCTION

My wife, Sandy, and I were researching and putting together a rough draft on our book, *All About Paul*. Paul was our Lord Jesus Christ's pick to be His apostle to the Gentiles. Sandy suggested that we take a breather and step back from this project for a while. She said, "We will interrupt Paul and give you an opportunity to look through your old family devotions for your book." Well, I did, but I wasn't pleased with the fact that the devotions just didn't seem current. The pandemic, the turmoil in our country, the riots, fires, and devastating hurricanes had left so many battered and bruised, emotionally, physically, and above all spiritually. I remarked to Sandy about what I had written previously and how I felt about it. Sandy encouraged, "Write about what is happening now. Write about hope, faith, and trust. These things are more important now than ever before. Write for such a time as this."

Well, I sat at the kitchen table and wandered through my Bible till my eyes fell on Ecclesiastes chapter three. It talks about there being a season to everything under heaven.

So was created *Interrupted Seasons*. The devotions are situational stories about the pandemic, disruptions, difficulties, and tragedies that have fallen on so many people during their seasons of life in 2020 and 2021.

There are forty devotions. Forty is a God number. The children of Israel wandered in the wilderness for forty years.

There was nothing normal about the seasons of their lives during this journey. Our Savior, Jesus, spent forty days in the wilderness too. His season was one of prayer, praise, and then temptation. He fought the devil and won. His strength was the Scriptures, which He used to let His adversary know that the heavenly Father is in control.

These devotions, although they bring to mind interruptions, hardships, and uncertainties of the seasons of our lives, still all point us towards the strength of the heavenly Father, the love we receive from our dear Savior, Jesus Christ, and the encouragement and support we receive when we call on the Holy Spirit.

For such a time as this!

1

My dear brothers and sisters, don't be fooled. Every good present and every perfect gift comes from above, from the Father who made the sun, moon, and stars. The Father doesn't change like the shifting shadows produced by the sun and the moon.

James 1:16-17

INTERRUPTED

One evening you sit down at the supper table. You've said the mealtime prayer, and you are just ready to take your first forkful of food when the doorbell rings. Somebody at the door has interrupted your meal. Or you are in bed fast asleep when the telephone rings. Somebody has interrupted your quiet rest time. Everybody has experienced interruptions, and it often involves a change of plans. It's just a fact of life. It happens.

What plans were you making in 2020 or 2021? Maybe it was a cruise to the Caribbean in March, or your daughter's graduation in May, or a baseball weekend with your favorite team, or a couple of weeks at the cabin. How did all that work out?

The Coronavirus (or COVID-19) is a dangerous virus that came from China, and it has changed our lives in so many ways. We have had to adapt to a "new normal." Shaking hands has given way to elbow and fist bumps. Wearing protective masks and personal distancing are now expected of us. Dining in restaurants and shopping in some stores is difficult. We hear people lamenting, "Life will never be the same again."

Yes, our whole lives have been interrupted. We have had to change or cancel our plans. There is not one person in the world who has not felt the effects of the pandemic. It's affected our work, travel, leisure, and family activities. Jobs are lost, businesses are closed, and many people are suffering financially.

But do you know what? Through all the uncertainty and through all of the chaos in our daily lives, there is something, and ultimately somebody, that never changes. It is the love of God for us in Christ Jesus. God comforts us in His Word that "Jesus Christ is the same yesterday, today, and forever" (Hebrews 13:8). And then we have God's promise when He tells us, "I will never abandon you or leave you" (Hebrews 13:5).

Although we have experienced a "new normal," and our lives have been interrupted, in faith, we believe that God will always be with us to watch over us, and protect us, and keep us safe. Let's hear the comforting words from God recorded in Psalm 23:

> The Lord is my shepherd. I am never in need. He makes me lie down in green pastures. He leads me beside peaceful waters. He renews my soul. He guides me along the paths of righteousness for the sake of his name. Even though I walk through the dark valley of death, because you are with me, I fear no harm. Your rod and your staff give me courage. You prepare a banquet for me while my enemies watch. You anoint may head with oil. My cup overflows. Certainly, goodness and mercy will stay close to me all the days of my life, and I will remain in the Lord's house for days without end.

REFLECTIONS: How has your life been interrupted lately? How does it feel when somebody interrupts you when you are talking? What are some examples of good and bad interruptions that have happened to you?

PRAYER: Dear Lord God, we thank you for interrupting our lives with goodness and mercy. Help us to see you at work within us so that we may show your love to everybody around us. It is the name of Jesus that we ask this. Amen.

FOR FURTHER READING: Ephesians 1:13-23.

2

Although you have never seen Christ, you love him. You don't see him now, but you believe in him. You are extremely happy with joy and praise that can hardly be expressed in words as you obtain the salvation that is the goal of your faith.

1 Peter 1:8-9

INVISIBLE ENEMIES

In the year 2020, we have been attacked by an invisible enemy. It is called Coronavirus (or COVID-19). It has caused many changes in our lives. Businesses, schools, and many gatherings have been closed for a time. It has been very upsetting for many. Parents are concerned, children are scared, and many have died from it. You can't see the virus, and you can't touch it, but it is still there, just the same. Regardless of who you are, it is upsetting our lives.

There is another invisible enemy that has been around since the beginning of time. The devil is very real. You can't see him, and you can't touch him, but he is working every day to do us harm. He is the reason we have so many bad things in our lives. Just think about what is going on in our world. Not only do we have to contend with this pandemic virus, but we also see hatred against one another. Hatred leads to riots, rebellion, and harm. The devil (or Satan) tempts us, confuses our minds, and tries very hard to lead us away from Jesus. The Bible warns us about him with these words: "Keep your mind clear, and be alert. Your opponent the devil is prowling around like a roaring lion as he looks for someone to devour. Be firm in the faith and resist him, knowing that other believers throughout the world are going through the same kind of suffering" (1 Peter 5:8-9).

What is the answer to all of this? After months at "warp speed," we have been given several COVID-19 vaccines that will keep us from getting the virus. We have the answer we have been waiting for.

God has an answer, too: fighting against the devil is Jesus, our Savior. Jesus' death on the cross won the victory over sin, death, and the devil, gaining eternal life for us. In the Bible, God tells us in Romans 6:23, "The gift that God freely gives is everlasting life." This is what we believe with all our hearts.

Even though we cannot see Jesus right now, we can hear what He has to say to us in His Word, which is the Bible. He tells us, "Every Scripture passage is inspired by God. All of them are useful for teaching, pointing out errors, correcting people, and training them for a life that has God's approval. They equip God's servants so that they are completely prepared to do good things" (2 Timothy 3:16-17).

Not only can we hear Jesus in the words of the Bible, but we can also see Him in His people of faith. When we do good things for others, Jesus tells us it's like we're doing it for Him. Jesus, the King in heaven, will say to His believers, "I was hungry, and you gave me something to eat. I was thirsty, and you gave me something to drink...Whatever you did for one of my brothers or sisters, no matter how unimportant they seemed, you did for me" (Matthew 25:35, 40).

So in times of trouble, like the nasty virus, or riots, or storm damage, or other times of need, you'll find that there are faithful Christians who are helping, giving, and sharing God's type of love. Jesus said, "I'm giving you a new commandment: Love each other in the same way that I have loved you. Everyone will know that you are my disciples because of your love for each other" (John 13:34-35).

We know that there are things in life that we can't see that may frighten us, like various illnesses or even the devil himself. There are also other things that we can see, like crime, and hatred, and riots, that may scare us too. The answer to all these things, seen or unseen, is Jesus, who promises that He will always be with us.

REFLECTIONS: What things do you find scary? What do you need so you won't be scared anymore? How can you help others not to be scared?

PRAYER: Dear Lord Jesus, we put ourselves in your loving, almighty, and helping hands. Your hands support and comfort us every day. Help us to come to you when we are scared, and keep us safe in your loving arms. We ask this in your holy name. Amen.

FOR FURTHER READING: Psalm 95:6-7.

3

God's riches, wisdom, and knowledge are so deep that it is impossible to explain his decisions or to understand his ways.

Romans 11:33

CRACK IT OPEN

It was Dad's turn to check Billy's lessons for the day. School was closed because of the pandemic, and in-home learning was required. Dad asked, "Billy, did you get your math done? And what about your reading assignment for English class? Don't forget to do your Bible reading for today too!"

Billy replied, "Yeah, about the Bible; I have so much to do today. This home school situation is so difficult for me; why do I have to read the Bible too?"

Dad pushed his chair a little closer next to Billy and said, "Let me tell you what Grandpa told me." Holding up a peanut in the shell, Dad said, "The Bible is like this peanut. You can see that the peanut has a hard shell on the outside. Of course, you can't eat the shell. It's very hard, and the taste is not good. So, in order to eat this peanut, you must 'crack it open' to get to the good-tasting nut inside."

Then Dad held up the Bible and continued, "Many Bibles have a beautiful cover. They look very nice sitting on the shelf or lying on the coffee table. And many homes have at least one

Bible somewhere in the house. But, like a peanut, the Bible will not do you any good until you 'crack it open.' And what do you find? We find something much better than a good-tasting peanut. You will find Words that God is speaking to you, or to anybody else who opens it and reads it."

The good news about Jesus is found there. In Romans 6:23, the verse says, "The gift that God freely gives is everlasting life found in Christ Jesus our Lord." Now, doesn't that sound great? Life forever with God in Heaven! Jesus earned us a place there by His perfect life and death on the cross. This gift is ours through nothing but faith. This is what we believe. This is why we love Jesus. This is the good news of the Bible.

But unless you "crack it open" and read it, or somebody like your Sunday school teacher, or your parents, or your grandparents teaches it to you, a closed Bible sitting on the table is like a peanut that is still in the shell. Unless the Bible is open and read, you will not know the comfort, the strength, and the love from God that is found there.

There are a lot of books that have been written during these days about the virus, riots, and such. They may be interesting, but none will give us the help and hope that we so need in these trying times like God's Word.

REFLECTIONS: Have you ever found something in the Bible that helped you? Have you ever wanted God to talk to you? Do you always trust that God will tell you the truth? How do you feel after reading the Bible?

PRAYER: We thank and praise you, dear Jesus, for giving us a book that tells us all about you and your love for us. What a special gift the Bible truly is! It helps us to keep ourselves close to you. Thank you, Jesus! Amen.

FOR FURTHER READING: Psalm 89:1-2.

4

God saved you through faith as an act of kindness [grace]. You had nothing to do with it. Being saved is a gift from God. It's not the result of anything you've done, so no one can brag about it.

Ephesians 2:8-9

ONLY $19.95

Dad was at home for the week. His company had closed temporally because of the pandemic lockdown. He was sitting at the kitchen table, working on the household budget and paying bills.

The chatter from his three sons in the next room caught his attention. "There is one for only $19.95," one son said. "I have found two," the second boy chimed in, "for $19.95 plus shipping and handling." The third son bragged, "I found five in my catalog."

It seems they were playing the suitcase game, each with a catalog, looking for items that were listed for sale at $19.95. Then they each made a list of the items in their suitcase, which is what they would take on a pretend journey. The boys were laughing and having a good time.

But it was time for morning devotions, and Dad had a bright idea. Maybe he could use the game they were playing as an example for the devotion.

So, Dad walked into the living room with a Bible in his hand and joined his sons as he sat down on the couch. He said, "I know of a much better deal than 'only $19.95.' It is absolutely *free*, and the benefits are far greater than any item in those catalogs. The deal is found in the Bible, and it is about Jesus. Then Dad opened the Bible and said, "Listen to this promise, as recorded in Romans 6:23, 'The gift that God freely gives is everlasting life found in Christ Jesus our Lord.'"

"Wow!" Dad exclaimed. "Isn't that great news? A gift is something that somebody freely gives us. It doesn't cost $19.95, or anything for that matter. It's absolutely free! And Jesus came to our world out of love for us. He was willing to live perfectly, in our place, because we just cannot do it ourselves. Then to top it off, he was willing to suffer the pain of the cross and die, to pay for all we have ever done wrong in our life. All of it was paid for by Jesus. He did it willingly, graciously, and freely, for you and for me. What a blessing!"

Then Dad continued, "And what do we get when we accept through faith what Jesus did for us? It's something better than any product we could buy for $19.95, or a hundred dollars, or even a million dollars! We will receive eternal life in heaven, with Jesus, in glory, in joy, in comfort, in security, without fear, or pain, or any reason to cry."

Dad paged to another place in the Bible. "Listen to this beautiful description of heaven God explains to us. In Revelation 7:16-17, we read, 'They will never be hungry or thirsty again. Neither the sun nor any burning heat will ever overcome them. The lamb [Jesus] in the center near the throne will be their shepherd. He will lead them to springs filled with the water of life, and God will wipe every tear from their eyes.'"

REFLECTIONS: What do you think heaven will be like? What happy things would you want to find in heaven? What do you think it will cost for you to get to heaven? What do you think it means when God tells us that we are saved by grace through faith alone?

PRAYER: Dear Jesus, we love you for being our Savior and promising us an eternal home in heaven. Help us to always trust your promises, and thank you for the free gift of salvation. What a blessing it is to know you in faith. In your name we pray, Jesus. Amen.

FOR FURTHER READING: Psalm 66:1-4.

5

I constantly remember you in my prayers night and day when I thank God, whom I serve with a clear conscience as my ancestors did. I remember your tears and want to see you so that I can be filled with happiness. I'm reminded of how sincere your faith is. That faith first lived in your grandmother Lois and your mother Eunice. I'm convinced that it also lives in you.

2 Timothy 1:3-5

TEACH THEM ABOUT JESUS

The COVID-19 pandemic has brought a harsh reality of lockdowns and closings into the households of many families. Moms and dads have had their places of employment shut down or temporarily closed. Because schools have closed, children have had to do their schoolwork at home. Even the younger children are locked out of daycare and preschool. Taking care of and teaching the youngest family members has never been so important.

Parents, have your children been taught to dress themselves, to tie their shoelaces, and bundle up when it's cold outside? Can they eat with knives, forks, and spoons, and can they drink from a glass? Do they know how to brush their teeth, wash their hands often, and wear masks when going outside? Can they count? Can they read a book? Do they know their ABCs? Even if they can't do all of these things now, you will teach them.

Another thing they should also be learning is about Jesus. Are you reading to them from the Bible so that they know the various stories? Have you taught them to memorize Bible verses?

Maybe they have learned this song about God, "Jesus loves me this I know, for the Bible tells me so." It's a very simple song, but it tells about our Savior's personal relationship with each individual child.

In the Bible, we meet a young pastor by the name of Timothy, who had learned about God from the time he was a very small boy from his grandmother, Lois, and his mother, Eunice. His teacher, the apostle Paul, wrote him a letter where he urged him, "Continue in what you have learned and found to be true. You know who your teachers were. From infancy you have known the Holy Scriptures. They have the power to give you wisdom so that you can be saved through faith in Christ Jesus" (2 Timothy 3:14-15).

Children need to learn about Jesus as soon as they can and continue to learn from the Bible for the rest of their life. And here are some words of encouragement for parents, "Train a child in the way he should go, and even when he is old he will not turn away from it" (Proverbs 22:6).

Start teaching your children when they are very young, even infants, about Jesus and the good news from the Bible. Read to them. Share with them. Share God's love with them. And let us all stay with Jesus, no matter what our age is. Having faith in our Savior is a personal thing, even for the very young. Then we too will be saved and will be with Jesus forever in heaven. Jesus tells us, "Go everywhere in the world, and tell everyone the good news. Whoever believes and is baptized will be saved" (Mark 16:15-16).

Thank and praise God as a family; love Him, share Him, and live for Him. "Jesus loves me, he will stay, close beside me all the way."

REFLECTIONS: Who has taught you about Jesus? How do you know that Jesus loves you? Do you think Jesus loves people who don't know about Him?

PRAYER: Dear Lord Jesus, help us to stay close to you always. Help us to love you more and show your love to others. Let us be the ones to share you with others who do not know you yet. In your holy name we ask it. Amen.

FOR FURTHER READING: Psalm 34:11-15.

6

Then Jesus went with the disciples to a place called Gethsemane. He said to them, "Stay here while I go over there and pray." He took Peter and Zebedee's two sons with him. He was beginning to feel deep anguish. Then he said to them, "My anguish is so great that I feel as if I'm dying. Wait here, and stay awake with me.

Matthew 26:36-38

A VERY SPECIAL GARDEN

Jenny's school had just sent all the students home because somebody in the fourth grade above Jenny had just gotten the new strange COVID-19 virus from China. No one knew much about it, except that it was dangerous and people who got it could die.

Jenny circled through the rooms of her home with nothing to do. Her mom handed her several spring seed catalogs. "Here, look through these and see what vegetables and flowers you might like to order with Dad," Mother said. "Thanks, Mom," she said. "I love our garden and can't wait to help Dad when planting time comes."

Mom sat down next to her daughter and paged through a catalog too. Mom said, "When spring comes, I also think of another garden. I think of the garden of Gethsemane. The season of Lent comes in the spring, and during Lent, we think of how Jesus prayed in that garden and was taken captive there."

Then mother continued, "Do you know that the garden of Gethsemane is still there in Israel? After more than two thousand years, it is still there. Tourists who visit the Holy Land usually make a stop at this garden, which is located on a hillside just outside of Jerusalem. Visitors are surprised when they see that it is actually a cemetery. But it is also a garden, just the same. Inside the fence, you'll find old olive trees, a scattering of flowers, and other plant life amongst the gravestones. It is a quiet and peaceful place, the perfect spot for Jesus to be in conversation with His Father in heaven, where He would be focused and undisturbed. What a wonderful experience it is to be in the very place where Jesus prayed so long ago!"

Mom continued, "It's right here in the Bible." She opened the family Bible to Mark 14:32 and read, "Then they came to a place called Gethsemane. He said to his disciples, 'Stay here while I pray.'"

In the springtime, perhaps we think about warmer weather or flowers. Have you ever thought about the garden of Gethsemane and what happened there? Just remember that Jesus was praying there the night before He would be put to death.

The season of Lent is a special time for any Christian. It reminds us of the suffering Jesus went through to gain for us the forgiveness of our sins. Jesus gives us peace with God the Father and promises us a home in heaven that's waiting for us, prepared for us by Jesus himself. In John 14:2, Jesus tells us, "My Father's house has many rooms…I'm going to prepare a place for you."

So the garden of Gethsemane is a very special place for people like you and me, who love our Savior with all our heart. It was there that Jesus' suffering began, ending on the cross, as He paid for our sins. Yes, Lord, we believe. Help us stay close to you always. And yes indeed, thank you, Lord Jesus, for loving us so much!

REFLECTIONS: Have you ever walked through a garden full of flowers? Have you thought about how God made the flowers and the seeds? Have you thought about how beautiful your eternal home in heaven must be?

PRAYER: Dear Jesus, we remember the garden, the cross, and the empty tomb. You did all this for us because of your deep love for us. We look forward to seeing our home for eternity in heaven. Thank you, Jesus, for giving us this wonderful promise. Amen.

FOR FURTHER READING: Psalm 103:1-6.

7

Because all people have sinned, they have fallen short of God's glory. They receive God's approval freely by an act of his kindness through the price Christ Jesus paid to set us free from sin.

Romans 3:23-24

SECRET SINS

Tommy and his family were in lockdown due to the virus. Mom sent him out of the house to play in the backyard. "Behave yourself now!" Mom smiled. Tommy headed straight to his treehouse fort and climbed up. He liked to play up high. As the afternoon wore on, it was time to come in and help with supper.

As he was in the bathroom washing his hands, he said, "Ouch, my finger hurts! Look here, Mom, I have scratched myself! I don't remember doing that." Mom looked at the scratch on his finger. "You did that when you were in your treehouse; you were so busy that you just didn't notice."

Sometimes we do things and are not aware of them either, nor do we remember them. Another time, Tommy bumped into a door and got a cut on his forehead. He wasn't hurt badly, but he cursed God's name. He hardly realized he had said it, but he did. He didn't even remember doing it a few minutes later, but God did.

In Tommy's house, there's a plaque on the wall that reads, "Jesus Christ is the head of this house; He's the unseen guest at every meal and the silent listener to every conversation." God hears all that we say, He sees *all* that we do, and He even knows what we are thinking. These forgotten, unnoticed sins are sometimes called *secret sins.*

What should we do about those secret sins that we can't even remember? We should ask for God's forgiveness, as we do with all our wrongs. And we should realize that God does indeed forgive us for Jesus' sake. Yes, God will forgive us, even all of those nasty little "secret sins."

King David was a faithful follower of God in the Old Testament time, but he did some wrong things too, as we all do. And David wrote in Psalm 19:12 about his secret sins that he had forgotten about. He asked God, "Who can notice every mistake? Forgive my hidden faults." Through Jesus, our sins are cleansed, made clean, and forgiven; yes, even those forgotten, secret sins.

So, it is indeed possible to get scratched or bruised and not even notice it at first. And it is also possible to sin without noticing it or even remembering it. But God knows. How many sins do we do in a lifetime? We surely could not remember them all, especially since some are secret sins that we barely remember at the time.

What a blessing it is to know that Jesus has paid for *all* sin with His suffering on the cross, even our secret sins too. St. Paul reminds us in 2 Corinthians 5:19, "God was using Christ to restore his relationship with humanity. He didn't hold people's faults against them." And God tells us in Jeremiah 31:34, "I will forgive their wickedness and I will no longer hold their sins against them." God won't keep bringing up our past sins; as far as He is concerned, it's like those sins never happened in the first place. How great is that?

There are a lot of things wrong in our world. With the virus, the protests, the riots, and the vandalism, it seems that there is so much hate going on. And none of us are perfect either. But God forgives all of our sins for Jesus' sake, and He promises to deliver us out of this wicked world in the life to come.

REFLECTIONS: Have you ever felt that you have done something so bad that God would never forgive you? Do you think that there are people who are so bad that God does not love them? How can you show others the blessings of God's forgiveness?

PRAYER: Thank you, Jesus, for forgiving *all* of my sins, even my secret sins. May your love and mercy guide me in all that I say and do. You are the steady influence and positive hope in my life. Thank you, Jesus. Amen.

FOR FURTHER READING: Psalm 103:1-4.

8

You are all God's children by believing in Christ Jesus. Clearly, all of you who were baptized in Christ's name have clothed yourselves with Christ. There are neither Jews nor Greeks, slaves nor free people, males nor females. You are all the same in Christ Jesus. If you belong to Christ, then you are Abraham's descendants and heirs, as God promised.

Galatians 3:26-29

DIFFERENT, BUT YET THE SAME

Because of the COVID-19 lockdown, we have had plenty of time this summer to do people-watching. We have seen on television the protests and have watched marches from the safety of our front steps. Even though they were wearing masks, bandanas, or scarves around their faces, you could tell that some people were short while others were tall; some had light-colored hair, and others had dark hair. Something was different with each person. That's the way it is with everyone.

On his first day of kindergarten, young Robbie had quite a shock. There were two girls in class that looked exactly the same! He had never seen twins before, and Susie and Sally were identical twins. They even dressed alike! Robbie couldn't tell them apart, and he was always afraid that he'd call them by the wrong name. But as the school year progressed, Robbie found that he could tell them apart because they had different personalities, along with a few other unique features. As much alike as Susie and Sally were, they were still very different people.

There are many things in this world that are different. We have different personalities. No two snowflakes are the same. Nobody's fingerprints will match anybody else's. Our individual voice patterns can identify us as sure as a fingerprint. Even the cloud formations in the sky are different from each other.

When you get to know people, you'll find even more differences in their likes and dislikes, and in the way they talk, and in how they think. So people differ greatly in how they look and in how they behave.

Yet, everybody is the same. St. Paul recorded these words from God, "Because all people have sinned, they have fallen short of God's glory" (Romans 3:23). Whether we are young or old, short or tall, light or dark, we are sinful. All of us do and say things we should not say or do, things that disappoint God and upset other people, so we all *absolutely need* Jesus Christ as our Savior. Jesus loves us equally. He wants everyone to live with Him in heaven someday. The Bible says, "He [God] wants all people to be saved and to learn the truth" (1 Timothy 2:4). That's why Jesus died on the cross. The Bible also tells us, "Christ died for us while we were still sinners. This demonstrates God's love for us" (Romans 5:8).

Whatever we look like, whoever we are, however we talk, we need Jesus, our only Savior from sin. And all of us who love Him in faith will live with Him in heaven forever. God gives us this beautiful promise in John 3:16, "God loved the world this way: He gave his only Son so that everyone who believes in him will not die [perish] but will have eternal life."

REFLECTIONS: How are you different from some of your friends? How are you the same? Do you feel you're better than somebody else because they're different than you?

PRAYER: Thank you, Jesus, for loving us *all*, no matter who we are or what we look like, or how different we are from each other. We who love you wait anxiously to meet you in heaven. There will be all kinds of people in your heaven— short, tall, different colored skins, and male and female. And all will be together, with you, in love. Amen.

FOR FURTHER READING: Psalm 100:1-5.

9

Don't say anything that would hurt another person. Instead speak only what is good that you can give help wherever it is needed. That way, what you say will help those who hear you. Don't give God's Holy Spirit any reason to be upset with you. He has put his seal on you for the day you will be set free from the world of sin. Get rid of your bitterness, hot tempers, anger, loud quarreling, cursing, and hatred. Be kind to each other, sympathetic, forgiving each other as God has forgiven you through Christ.

Ephesians 4:29-32

Be Careful What You Say

An older gentleman was sitting on a park bench. He heard some children approaching from behind. He couldn't see them, but he could hear what the two boys were saying.

The one boy said harshly, "Give me that blankety-blank dollar! I want it!" The other boy said, "But I found it. It's my dollar." The first boy cursed and swore at him and threatened to beat him up if he didn't give him that dollar. The second boy got scared and said, "Here, take it."

About that time, the boys came into view of the man on the bench. He wondered which boy was which. They were both wearing blue jeans and athletic shoes and had masks on due to the virus. He couldn't tell who said those nasty words.

Then one of the boys spoke again as they walked away. He said, "You are blankety-blank lucky you gave the dollar to me when you did!" Now the man knew which was which!

How you speak shows the type of person you are. God tells us in James 1:26, "If a person thinks that he is religious but can't control his tongue, he is fooling himself. That person's religion is worthless." If you want to know what kind of a person someone is, even though you don't know them or their name, just listen to what they say and how they say it. We show what is deep inside of us when we speak. If we speak with love, there must be love inside. But if we speak with hate and bitterness, then that is what must be inside.

What kind of words come from us? Are they loving words, words that honor God and make others feel good? We hope so! There are too many people in the world who often speak with bitterness and selfishness. So many people bring dishonor and shame to God and His holy name. Such bad language should *never* come from the lips of those who know about God's love in faith.

It says in 1 John 4:19, "We love because God first loved us." He even sent His Son to be our Savior. We want His generous kind of love to also flow from our hearts, our minds, and our mouths. We belong to God in faith, and we want our lives and words to show it.

REFLECTIONS: What situations might cause a person to use bad language? How do you feel when you hear people use bad language? How can we use our words to help people and make them feel good?

PRAYER: Dear Jesus, help me say things that are right and good that will bring glory to your name and will help others be closer to you. Thank you for the privilege of praying, praising, and giving thanks to you. Amen.

FOR FURTHER READING: Psalm 34:11-14.

Love isn't rude. It doesn't think about itself. It isn't irritable. It doesn't keep track of wrongs. It isn't happy when injustice is done, but it is happy with the truth. Love never stops being patient.

1 Corinthians 13:5-7a

PRETTY INSIDE

Billy's mom and dad were going out for the evening, so they asked Mollie Jo, the girl who lived across the street, to come over and stay with Billy while they were gone. She liked staying with Billy because he always had some sort of thing they could do together.

"Here, Billy; according to the directions, these two pieces go together," Mollie Jo said. She was showing him how to glue a model fighter jet together. She was being very kind and patient with the boy, who was somewhat clumsy and not very handy with craft projects and model glue. Besides, he was a little shy on top of it all.

All of a sudden, Billy looked up and smiled. Very quietly, he said to Mollie Jo, "You are awful pretty." Mollie Jo was surprised. She had known Billy ever since he was born, and he had never said anything like that before. "Oh, you can't mean that," she said, tugging at her mask. She was quite flustered and embarrassed. "You can't even see my face." "I mean, you are pretty on the *inside*, in a place you cannot see," Billy said sincerely.

Do you know what Billy meant? Since Mollie Jo was kind and helpful to him, he just knew that she was nice inside, in her heart, and in her mind.

Some people can be so beautiful on the outside but still be ugly on the inside. Next door to Billy lived a girl his age named Angelica. She had bright eyes, a big smile, white teeth, and long blonde hair, which sometimes had a ribbon on the side. At a distance, anyone would think she was something special.

The only problem was that Angelica was a selfish, spoiled child who thought she should always get her way. Sometimes she would stamp her feet and say mean and naughty things. Sometimes she would pout and throw things in anger. She was *not* pretty on the inside at all!

What kind of people are we? Are we pretty inside? We may be able to hide our true inside to many people. But you can never ever fool God! God doesn't look at us like most other people do. Most people look at us on the outside. They see what we look like, how we behave towards others, and what we say or do.

But God knows all things. One time, Simon Peter said to Jesus, "Lord, you know everything" (John 21:17). God looks at us on the inside. He even knows what we are thinking. The Bible says, "God does not see as humans see. Humans look at outward appearances, but the Lord looks into the heart" (1 Samuel 16:7).

No matter what we look like on the outside, we all can be pretty *inside*. Out of love for Jesus, and with the help of God, we can show others how beautiful God's love is on the inside of us. We want to be this way because Jesus has loved us so much that He died on the cross to save us from our sins. And Jesus says to us, "Love each other as I have loved you" (John 15:12). No matter how you look on the outside, when you show God's love to others, you are simply beautiful inside and out, through and through.

REFLECTIONS: Can you think of people you know who are pretty on the inside? How do they show you that they're pretty? Who do you know who isn't very pretty on the inside? Do you think that Jesus can make them pretty?

PRAYER: Lord, Jesus, help us to be pretty on the inside and to show it, just like you have shown your love for us. It is only with your help and guidance we can do this. We love you, Jesus, and want to share your love with others. Amen, Jesus. Amen.

FOR FURTHER READING: Psalm 147:1-7.

11

God...promised this Good News through his prophets in the Holy Scriptures. This Good News is about his Son, our Lord Jesus Christ. In his human nature he was a descendant of David. In his spiritual, holy nature he was declared the Son of God. This was shown in a powerful way when he came back to life. Through him we have received God's kindness and the privilege of being apostles who bring people from every nation to the obedience that is associated with faith. This is for the honor of his name. You are amongst those who have been called to belong to Jesus Christ.

Romans 1:2-6

HE SLEPT TOO

It was springtime, and the family was doing the annual yard clean-up. Dad had been laid off from work due to the virus. So to save some money, they were going to plant an extra big vegetable garden this year. All of the family was pitching in to do the yard work and prepare the vegetable garden and flower beds for planting.

"I'm so tired," young Mark said after being outside all day. He was only five years old, and he was really tired. He leaned up against his mother on the couch, just quietly drifting off to sleep in the evening darkness.

We all get tired, don't we? Our bodies can only go so long, and then we have to get some rest. It's that way with all people, no matter how old we are.

It was also that way with Jesus. He got tired and slept at night like we do. The Bible tells about the time when Jesus was so tired He went to sleep in the bottom of a boat. "As they were sailing along, Jesus fell asleep" (Luke 8:23). What was so surprising about it is that the boat was in a terrible storm, and it was almost ready to sink. "A violent windstorm came up. The waves were breaking into the boat so that it was quickly filling up" (Mark 4:37). Finally, in fear for their lives, His disciples woke Jesus up and asked for His help. He said to the wind and the wild sea, "Be still, absolutely still" (Mark 4:39). And all of a sudden the wind stopped blowing, the sea became calm, the rain stopped, and it was all quiet!

That story tells us something very special about our Lord Jesus. He was certainly human because He got tired and slept just like we do. But He was also the Son of God! How could any man say, "Be still, absolutely still," to the wind and rain and have it stop? No ordinary person could do that. But then, Jesus was and is no ordinary man. He didn't have a human father, but God was His Father. That is why Jesus had the power to calm the winds of that terrible storm at sea. St. Paul explains this, "All of God lives in Christ's body" (Colossians 2:9).

Jesus also has the power to save us from our sins. We can't be perfect, no matter how hard we try. But Jesus was perfect in our place. He died on the cross to pay for our wrongs. When He said from the cross, "It is finished" (John 19:30), everything necessary for our salvation was finished. He rose to life again in three days. That is what we believe with all our hearts. Because of what He did for us, we shall be with Him in heaven. "Whoever believed in the Son [Jesus] has eternal life" (John 3:36).

REFLECTIONS: How do you feel when there is a bad thunder and lightning storm? What do you think Jesus' disciples were afraid of when that unexpected storm came up? Do we ever have trouble trusting Jesus when we feel threatened?

PRAYER: Thank you, Jesus, for being who you are, both man and God. And thank you, Jesus, for being our Savior and our friend. We are so blessed to know you in faith and love. Amen.

FOR FURTHER READING: Psalm 24:1-2, 7-10.

12

My son, do not forget my teachings, and keep my commands in mind, because they will bring you long life, good years, and peace. Do not let mercy and truth leave you. Fasten them around your neck. Write them on the tablet of your heart. Then you will find favor and much success in the sight of God and humanity. Trust the LORD with all your heart, and do not rely on your own understanding. In all your ways acknowledge him, and he will make your paths smooth.

Proverbs 3:1-6

WHAT'S A PENNY WORTH?

Dad had just finished moving his office in the storage room of the garage. His company had sent their employees home to work during the COVID-19 virus.

"Can I come in to see your new office?" Bobby asked. "Sure, come on in," Dad said. "This is where I'm going to be working every day until this pandemic is over, and I can go back to my office downtown."

Bobby looked around at everything. His dad had made a desk out of some sawhorses and plywood. He had his computer and printer all set up, his comfortable office chair was in its place, and there were several baskets of file folders sitting off to the side. But then, Bobby's eyes got as big as saucers when he spotted the huge glass jar of pennies sitting beside his dad's desk. "Wow! Where did you get all those pennies?" Bobby exclaimed.

"I have been saving them for many years," Dad explained. Bobby replied, "They are just pennies. You can't buy hardly anything for just a penny." Dad answered, "I always pick up lost coins when I find them. Do you have any idea why I do this?" Bobby thought for a few moments and said, "No, I don't." Dad smiled and explained, "Here, let me show you. Look at this penny. Do you see the words that are inscribed on it?" Bobby squinted as he held up the penny. Bobby stated, "It says 'In God We Trust' on it." Dad said, "Every coin, including pennies, has the words 'In God We Trust' on it. So every time I pick up coins from the ground, even if it is just a penny, I am reminded to trust in God. This is not a bad reminder, huh?" Bobby looked the coin over carefully. "Hmmm; I never thought of it that way before," he said thoughtfully.

Trusting in God is a very important thing to do in our lives, especially in these times of the pandemic. St. Paul records these words from God: "We have peace with God because of what our Lord Jesus Christ has done" (Romans 5:1). So many people have stress, tension, and fear in their life. They are afraid of so many things in life, and their life is so unsure and unstable. To know the love God has for us is so comforting and peaceful. St. Paul records some more words from God: "We're not ashamed to have this confidence, because God's love has been poured into our hearts by the Holy Spirit, who has been given to us" (Romans 5:5).

Christians are never alone, but God (Father, Son, and Holy Spirit) is with us every day, watching out for us, encouraging us, protecting us, and sharing His love for us. What could be better than that? So, whatever in our lives assures us of God's love for us, it is special indeed. Even if it is just a penny in a jar or in our pocket, we can look at it and see those four very comforting words: "In God we trust."

REFLECTIONS: What are the things that remind you to trust in God? Have you ever been tempted to trust something other than God? How can you encourage other people to trust in God?

PRAYER: Thank you, Lord, for the simple reminders to trust you with everything. We need these types of reminders about trust. We love you, God, and we trust you. It is in your name Jesus, we pray. Amen.

FOR FURTHER READING: Psalm 138:1-8.

13

*Certainly, all who are guided by God's Spirit are God's children.
You haven't received the spirit of slaves that leads you into fear
again. Instead, you have received the spirit of God's adopted
children by which we call out, "Abba! Father!" The Spirit himself
testifies with our spirit that we are God's children. If we are his
children, we are also God's heirs. If we share in Christ's suffering
in order to share his glory, we are heirs together with him. I consider
our present sufferings insignificant compared to the glory that will
soon be revealed to us.*

Romans 8:14-18

WHO'S CHILD ARE YOU?

It wasn't a typical Sunday. Everyone was outside, wearing masks,
and sitting a distance apart in the church parking lot. The pastor
preached from the back of a pickup truck. The community was
in lockdown due to the virus.

After the service, a kindly old gentleman asked, "And
whose boy are you?" The child answered and told him his
name. "Oh, you are Henry's boy," he stated. "Yep," the boy
replied. "I'm Henry's boy, but I'm also God's child." The man
replied, "You are right," and smiled. He continued, "But you
know what? I'm a child of God, just like you. That makes us
brothers in God's family." The boy replied, "We talked about
that in Sunday school today. We are one family in Jesus."

You know it's true. We are also children of God and part of God's family. All who believe in Jesus Christ as Savior are brothers and sisters in faith. And as we learn more and more from God's Word over the years, that faith grows and becomes stronger. So yes, we are children of God in faith. St. Paul gives us some good words to remember: "All who are guided by God's Spirit are God's children" (Romans 8:14).

Do you know what makes being in God's family so special? For one thing, we are forgiven of all our wrongs. Jesus earned that forgiveness for us when He died on the cross to pay for our sins. It says in the Bible, "The gift that God freely gives is everlasting life found in Christ Jesus our Lord" (Romans 6:23). And when we leave this world in death, then we will go to be with God and all the family of believers in heaven, in a beautiful home that Jesus has made especially for us. How wonderful that will be!

And even now, as members of God's family of faith, we have our dear Lord Jesus looking after us and providing for us. Jesus sends His angels to protect us from danger. He blesses us with good food, warm homes, and parents who love us.

Oh yes, bad things still happen to us. And when temptation and troubles come our way, God helps us to handle them. God promises us in the Bible, "I will never abandon you or leave you. So we can confidently say, 'The Lord is my helper, I will not be afraid. What can mortals do to me?'" (Hebrews 13:5-6). Isn't it nice to know we are God's children in faith?

REFLECTIONS: Who are the members of your family here on earth? Can you name some of the family members in God's family? What kind of comfort do you have by being a member of God's family?

PRAYER: Thank you, heavenly Father, for your love and many blessings. Thank you for adopting me as your child through faith in Jesus. We are blessed to be part of God's family of believers. Thank you. We pray in His name. Amen

FOR FURTHER READING: Matthew 6:9-13.

14

Whoever is a believer in Christ is a new creation. The old way of living has disappeared. A new way of living has come into existence. God has done all this. He has restored our relationship with him through Christ, and has given us this ministry of restoring relationships. In other words, God was using Christ to restore his relationship with humanity. He didn't hold people's faults against them, and he has given us this message of restored relationships to tell others. Therefore, we are Christ's representatives, and through us God is calling you. We beg you on behalf of Christ to become reunited with God. God had Christ, who was sinless, take our sin so that we might receive God's approval through him.

2 Corinthians 5:17-21

PASS IT ON

The family could not go out to eat for the birthday meal because the restaurants were closed due to the virus. So Mom cooked a meal at home. It was a special fried chicken dinner that Mom had prepared for Leon. It was his favorite meal, with mashed potatoes, biscuits, and country gravy. When the chicken platter was passed to Leon, he took several pieces and began to eat right away. My goodness, was he ever hungry!

Dad said to him, "Leon, haven't you forgotten something?" Leon thought for a moment. "Oh yes," he said. "Thanks, Mom, for the great chicken! I love fried chicken!" Dad continued, "And we haven't thanked God yet for the meal either."

So the family joined in the table prayer, *"Bless us, O Lord, and these thy gifts which we are about to receive from thy bounty; through Christ our Lord. Amen."* "You forgot something else too," Dad reminded him. "You forgot to pass the chicken platter along." Oops! Leon felt so foolish, and he quickly passed the dish on to the next person at the table.

That's not such an unusual thing to happen now, is it? We often become so involved in our own personal interests and wants that we forget to say "thank you" or to pass things along to others who would enjoy them as much as we do.

Do you know the same thing can happen with Jesus? News about Jesus and His love for us was shared with us by someone in our lives. Otherwise, we might have never known about our Savior, His love, His forgiveness, and our heavenly home. For many, it was our parents who first shared Jesus with us. Maybe you remember a special Sunday school teacher or a pastor that made the good news of Jesus so clear and real to you. Maybe it was a friend or neighbor who first told you about the cross, the resurrection, and God's love for you. Or maybe you picked up a Bible that somebody gave you, and the love of God almost radiated from the pages.

Did you remember to say "thank you?" This gift of love, Jesus, is the most special thing a person can share with somebody. We could give someone a million dollars, but that would not bring them eternal life. We could give them a large, beautiful home, but that would not bring them forgiveness of their sins. Only the good news about Jesus can bring lasting blessings that will help us and keep us forever and ever. Did you remember to say "thank you" to whoever first told you about Jesus? Did you thank God that somebody, sometime, somewhere shared Jesus with you? And have you remembered to pass it on?

The birthday boy, Leon, was so interested in tasting the chicken that he forgot to pass the platter on to the others at the table. I hope none of us forget to pass along the news about Jesus. It could be easy to become so wrapped up in all the blessings we receive through faith in Jesus that we could just keep Him for ourselves and not remember others. *Everybody* needs forgiveness and love from Jesus, just as much as we do.

The Bible tells us that Jesus died and rose again for all. Jesus said, "So wherever you go, make disciples of all nations: Baptize them in the name of the Father, and of the Son, and of the Holy Spirit. Teach them to do everything I have commanded you" (Matthew 28:19-20).

Any time is a good time to thank God for all our blessings. It is also a good time to thank those who have shared Jesus with us. And anytime is a good time to *pass on* the good news about Jesus to others.

REFLECTIONS: Is there a special person in your life that talks to you about Jesus? Can you think of somebody who doesn't know Jesus? What can you do to bring the good news of Jesus to others?

PRAYER: Dear Jesus, thank you for giving me the beautiful message of salvation and the knowledge of your love through your Holy Word. Give me the courage, give me the words, and give me the willingness to share you, Jesus, with others. I ask it in your name. Amen.

FOR FURTHER READING: Psalm 145:1-9.

15

We were not completely wiped out. His compassion is never limited. It is new every morning. His faithfulness is great. My soul can say, 'The LORD is my lot in life; that is why I find hope in him.' The LORD is good to those who wait for him, to anyone who seeks help from him. It is good to continue to hope and wait silently for the LORD to save us.

Lamentations 3:22b-26

RAINBOW

The summer of 2020 was not an ordinary summer. The pandemic was spreading throughout the country. The Gulf States were preparing for the hurricane season.

The hurricane was due to reach land within hours, and the water was rising by inches on the small country farm. Even though John and Sarah were retired and by themselves, they loved the place. They had raised their four children there and had no thoughts of ever moving.

"You have to go now," the deputy sheriff in the boat told John and Sarah. "But we have lived here a long time," John replied. "When we lost our home last time, I built it up on pillars, a long way off the ground. See how high the steps are?" The deputy looked at the house. It was indeed about twelve feet off the ground, secured on the pillars cemented into the ground. Indeed it was very well built. "But I have my orders," he told the couple. "You are vulnerable, and you have to get into the boat and come with me." "Oh, no!" Sarah cried out. "What about our chickens, the dog, and cats, our pig, and Rosie, our cow. They are all going to drown!" she cried. John hugged her tight. "God will watch out for them," he encouraged her. "I have opened all the doors and gates so they can escape when the wind comes, and the water gets high." So John and Sarah reluctantly climbed into the boat.

It was two weeks to the day when John and Sarah returned to their farm. The hurricane was a very bad one, and there wasn't much left of this little farmstead. The orchard was gone, as well as the old shed and the barn, and no animals were in sight. But the house was still standing. The trees in the yard were all gone. The ground was still muddy and wet. A rain shower had just passed over. John and Sarah, their eyes wet with tears, stood quietly by the car as they looked over the devastation that lay before them. With not much to say, John pointed to the clouds in the distance. "Look, Sarah, a rainbow," he said.

Sarah laughed and pointed to the house. She said, "There are the chickens and the pig high on the porch of the house." The dog and cats walked out of the open door, and behind the doorway stood Rosie, the cow. "See, I told you that God would take care of the animals," John said.

Yes, God keeps His promises. Do you remember from the Bible how the rainbow started? God promised to send the rainbow after the great flood to show Noah and all of us today that He will never destroy the whole world by water again. Moses records this covenant or promise from God, "God said, 'This is the sign of the promise I am giving to you and every living being that is with you for generations to come. I will put my rainbow in the clouds to be a sign of my promise to the earth. Whenever I form clouds over the earth, a rainbow will appear in the clouds. Then I will remember my promise to you and every living animal. Never again will water become a flood to destroy all life'" (Genesis 9:12-15).

The rainbow that brightly shines and the colors from a sunset all remind us of the beauty and wonder of God's creation. The Lord made such a perfect world. If it hadn't been spoiled by sin, we would now be living in a paradise. But thanks be to Jesus, who paid for our sins on the cross, that in heaven we will know even more beauty and pleasure than a lovely sunset can bring.

John and Sarah smiled. They knew that God had been watching over them and protected their home and property. He even kept the animals safe! So they bowed their heads and thanked God for blessing them so much.

REFLECTIONS: Can you think of a time when God kept you safe? How are the ways He keeps you safe? Do you think God is with you even when you sleep?

PRAYER: Heavenly Father, thank you for protecting me and my loved ones and keeping us safe. In your strength and love, we are safe and secure. Continue to be with us always throughout our lives. It is in Jesus' name we pray. Amen.

FOR FURTHER READING: Psalm 148:1-7a.

16

Thank God that he gives us the victory through our Lord Jesus Christ. So, then, brothers and sisters, don't let anyone move you off the foundation of your faith. Always excel in the work you do for the Lord. You know that the hard work you do for the Lord is not pointless.

1 Corinthians 15:57-58

FLIPPING PANCAKES

A father and his son were attending an event at their church. It was being held in the parking lot because of the COVID-19 virus restrictions. A missionary from Africa was there to talk about his work in the country of Sudan. It was very interesting. He even had some native masks, spears, and other items made by the people there.

On the way home, the son said, "I could never serve God like that missionary does. I am too shy to stand up in front of people and give a talk. And I don't know any other language besides English, and I am not even very good with that."

Dad replied, "Well, you know, there are lots of ways that we can serve God. Not everyone can be a pastor or a missionary." He continued. "In fact, I serve God by flipping pancakes."

"What do you mean by 'flipping pancakes'?" The boy asked.

Dad explained to his son, "Just remember that our church normally has a monthly Men's Bible Breakfast. Either the pastor or one of the church elders leads in a short Bible study. But what really gets the men to attend is the great breakfast that is provided. I help out each month by flipping pancakes in the kitchen. The food is always great, and about fifty men attended every first Saturday of the month. Hopefully, we'll be starting up again after the pandemic is over."

Then Dad continued, "You know, there are a lot of ways to serve God and help others in need. The Bible has many verses that encourage us to 'love one another.' God tells us, 'Live in love as Christ also loved us. He gave His life for us as an offering and sacrifice, a soothing aroma to God' (Ephesians 5:2). God also tells us, 'Dear friends, we must love each other because love comes from God. Everyone who loves has been born from God and knows God'" (1 John 4:7).

Father and son continued their conversation about serving others in love. Dad said, "Do you remember last winter when we shoveled the snow from the walk of the elderly lady down the street? We didn't ask her for any money. She lives all by herself and doesn't have much money. We just did it out of Christian love. And remember when Bob from church was hurt in that car accident last year? Many of the church members got together and helped him finish the garage he was building. So you see, there are all kinds of ways to serve God and show His kind of love. I think you know what I am talking about."

"I guess you are right," the son replied. "I can serve God too, maybe not as a missionary, but I can still talk about Jesus and the cross, and I'm sure there are many other ways too. Maybe I can help you flip pancakes at the Men's Bible Breakfast when it starts up again."

REFLECTIONS: What are some of the ways that you can serve God? Can you think of others who are serving God in your church or community? What does it mean that we serve God when we serve others?

PRAYER: Help us, dear Jesus, to show your kind of love for you and others by all that we do or say. Give us opportunities to share your love every day. Guide us and direct us in our lives of service to you. In your name, Jesus, we ask it. Amen.

FOR FURTHER READING: Psalm 34:11-15, 17-19.

17

I don't do the good I want to do. Instead, I do the evil that I don't want to do…What a miserable person I am! Who will rescue me from my dying body? I thank God that our Lord Jesus Christ rescues me!

Romans 7:19, 24-25a

MOSQUITOES AND WEEDS

"Don't forget to wear your masks, you two," Mom yelled from the back kitchen door. The governor had ordered that everybody had to wear masks. This virus from China had everybody worried. Nobody had any idea how serious or contagious it was.

Nine-year-old Amy pulled the mask up over her nose as she helped her Dad pull weeds out of the garden. She would pull a weed or two and then slap a mosquito. This happened again and again. After a while, she asked Dad, "Why did God make mosquitoes and weeds?" That is a good question. Why did God make them?

We have to go back to the time when God made the world for the answer. The Bible says, "And God saw everything that he had made and that it was very good" (Genesis 1:31). So when God made the world, the animals, plants, and insects were all good. Originally weeds were not a problem, nor were mosquitoes.

It was not until Adam and Eve first sinned that things got out of control. As a punishment to them, God cursed the ground. This is how the Bible describes it: "The ground will grow thorns and thistles for you, and you will eat wild plants. By the sweat of your brow, you will produce food to eat until you return to the ground, because you were taken from it. You are dust, and you will return to dust" (Genesis 3:18-19).

So now, because Adam and Eve disobeyed God (and way too often, you and I do too), the ground is cursed, and weeds get out of control. They grow where we don't want them to, and they often grow faster than other plants in our garden.

And mosquitoes are a problem too. They didn't always bite and pester. But now, because of sin in the world, mosquitoes are a real problem.

But don't be discouraged! There is a time coming when weeds and mosquitoes will no longer be problems for us. And things like pandemics, riots, and hate will be no more. It will all be gone, thanks to our Savior, Jesus Christ. Jesus died on the cross and paid for all our sins. When we believe this in faith, then we are forgiven for all of our sins, and we have God's promise that we will be with Him in heaven someday. Jesus said to the thief on the cross who believed in Him, "I can guarantee this truth: today you will be with me in paradise" (Luke 23:43).

In that wonderful place, if indeed there are any weeds or mosquitoes, they will no longer be a problem in the paradise of heaven. In Revelation 7:16-17, God gives us a brief description of heaven: "They will never be hungry or thirsty again. Neither the sun nor any burning heat will ever overcome them. The Lamb [Jesus] in the center near the throne will be their shepherd. He will lead them to springs filled with the water of life, and God will wipe every tear from their eyes."

Thank God for that wonderful home! Praise His holy name! And we always want to remember the wonderful promise that Jesus tells us, "God loved the world this way: he gave his only Son so that everyone who believes in him will not die [perish] but will have eternal life" (John 3:16). A long time ago, Thomas R. Taylor wrote these words: "I'm but a stranger here, heaven is my home; earth is a desert drear, heaven is my home. How great that will be!"

REFLECTIONS: What makes you happy? What are some of the things that you find annoying? What are some of the things you would like to see in heaven?

PRAYER: We can hardly wait to be with you, Jesus, in your perfect, wonderful, glorious heavenly home. This world is not perfect, nor are we. We pray that you will bring us safely to your perfect home in heaven. We ask it in your name, Jesus. Amen.

FOR FURTHER READING: Psalm 8:1-9.

18

God has shown us his love by sending his only Son into the world so that we could have life through him. This is love: not that we have loved God, but that he loved us and sent his Son to be the payment for our sins. Dear friends, if this is the way God loved us, we must also love each other.

1 John 4:9-11

CAMPING OUT WITH GOD

The COVID-19 virus has changed many plans for a lot of people. The family had planned a theme park vacation, but that couldn't happen. So, Dad and Mom decided this might be a good time to take a camping vacation instead. They hadn't gone camping since their little daughter Amy was born four years ago, and there was a state forest only a couple hours away.

The little girl was having a good time checking out all the sights, sounds, and smells of the forest. What an awesome experience it was learning about nature!

But that all changed under the cover of darkness. There was no light, and Amy heard lots of sounds she never heard before. So she cried, "Mommy! Mommy! I'm afraid!" "Mommy and Daddy are right here," Mom said as she hugged her. Dad added, "You don't have to be afraid of anything. We'll protect you."

"I wish Jesus was here," the little girl said as she snuggled in between her parents. "He is here with us," Mom assured her. "I thought you said Jesus would be with Grandma in the nursing home." Amy reminded her mother.

"Well, there is something special about Jesus," Mom replied. "He is not like you and me, who can be only one place at a time. Jesus can be everywhere at the same time." "How can that be?" Amy puzzled. "I don't know how He does it," Mom answered. "But that is what the Bible says about Him. God says, 'Don't be afraid, because I am with you. Don't be intimidated; I am your God. I will strengthen you. I will help you. I will support you with my victorious right hand (Isaiah 41:10).'"

Dad continued, "Jesus can do anything because He is God. Jesus says, 'All authority in heaven and on earth has been given to me (Matthew 28:18).' And Jesus also reassures us, 'And remember that I am always with you until the end of time (Mathew 28:20).'" Mom added, "So the Lord Jesus can be at the nursing home watching over Grandma, and He can also be here protecting us." She concluded, "Do you see how well He cares for us?" The mother tucked the covers tightly around Amy and both her parents gave her a kiss.

"I feel better now," Amy said with a confident smile. Now all the scary dark trees and frightening animal sounds didn't bother Amy. She was able to go to sleep, knowing Jesus was by her side.

The Lord Jesus Christ is everywhere at once. He is all-powerful and all-knowing. He is truly loving and merciful. We know His love very well because He came to be our Savior from sin. This is what we believe with all our hearts.

REFLECTIONS: What kinds of things do you find scary? Has a new experience ever frightened you? What gives you comfort when you are scared?

PRAYER: Thank you, Lord Jesus, for always being close to us. What a comfort and joy that is, especially in these difficult times. And we look forward to being with you in heaven, where we will be safe and happy all the time and forever. In your name, Jesus. Amen.

FOR FURTHER READING: Psalm 4:1, 4-8.

19

Never worry about anything. But in every situation let God know what you need in prayers and requests while giving thanks.

Philippians 4:6

THANKFUL TO WHOM

It was the first day of class after weeks of lockdown at home due to the virus. Everyone was wearing masks, their desks were apart, and the teacher stood a great distance away from the students. "I'm so grateful to have you here," she said. "Let's take time to write down a list of the things that we are grateful for today."

On the way home, Bill and Robbie compared their lists. Bill got a bicycle that he thanked his parents for. Then he was able to go camping and fishing with his dad for a week; he was thankful to his dad for that. He also got new tennis shoes and a backpack, and he was thankful to his grandparents for that.

The other boy, Robbie, was thankful to God that when his mom was very sick with the Coronavirus, she had completely recovered. He was thankful to God that his dad still had his job. And he was so glad that his grandparents were healthy and well.

Can you see a difference in their lists? Robbie thanked God for what others received, while Bill didn't look beyond himself.

We read in the Bible that Jesus came upon ten men who had a very bad skin disease. Jesus saw this and healed all ten of them as they walked along the road. This was one of God's miracles, and it meant a whole new life for them. But what happened? Only one man turned around and returned to Jesus to say "thank you." Jesus asked him, "Weren't ten men made clean? Where are the other nine?" (Luke 17:17). Certainly, all of them were thankful that they were healed. But only one of them thought it was important to go back and say "thank you" to Jesus.

To whom are we thankful? Of course, we are glad when people help other people. And we should remember to thank others who help us. But let's also remember *who* provides people to help us; it is God! Only God knows what we all need. Only God is able to answer all our prayers for help. He works through the doctors and nurses to bring us good health. God guides Christian parents in caring for their children. It is God who sends the rain, the sun and makes the seeds grow to a fine harvest. He is the real source of all that is good and wonderful in our world. He even sent Jesus to save us from our sins! What a huge blessing that is!

Both Bill and Robbie were thankful for things, as they should be. Both had been blessed in different ways. In the Bible, God tells us, "Every good present and every perfect gift comes from above, from the Father who made the sun, moon, and stars" (James 1:17).

Many of the psalms in the Bible also talk about being thankful to God, for example, "Give thanks to the LORD because he is good, because his mercy endures forever...Let them give thanks to the LORD because of his mercy" (Psalm 107:1, 15).

We would certainly say "thank you" to our relatives, friends, and others in many situations; however, we need to remember to thank God above all. The Lord is good to us, and He makes all good things happen. So, we offer Him our sincerest thanks and praise.

REFLECTIONS: Can you think of some things for which you are thankful? Do you like it when people say "thank you" to you? Do you always remember to say "thank you" to other people?

PRAYER: Dear Jesus, help me to always say "thank you" to other people. Help me always remember to give thanks to you for your love and your many blessings. You are the source of all our wonderful blessings. All praise and honor be to your holy name, Jesus. Amen.

FOR FURTHER READING: Psalm 107:1, 8-9.

20

This is the testimony: God has given us eternal life, and this life is found in his Son. The person who has the Son has this life. The person who doesn't have the Son of God doesn't have this life. I've written this to those who believe in the Son of God so that they will know that they have eternal life. We are confident that God listens to us if we ask for anything that has his approval. We know that he listens to our requests. So we know that we already have what we ask him for.

1 John 5:11-15

WHY DID HE SAY NO?

Four-year-old Sam came running up to his father. "Daddy, will you please open this bottle for me?" "Sorry Sam, I won't do it," his dad replied.

Now, why do you suppose Sam's dad said "No?" Was it because he was a mean man who refused to do anything helpful for his child? That was not the reason at all. This dad was kind and loving and was always willing to help his family in any way he could.

Was it because Sam's dad was too weak to open the bottle? That is not the reason because he was a big man with very strong hands. He certainly could have opened the bottle if he had wanted to. Or maybe it was the third bottle of orange soda in a row that young Sam wanted to drink. But that was wrong too. It was not a bottle of orange soda that Sam wanted his dad to open.

What Sam wanted his dad to open was a bottle of drain cleaner from under the kitchen sink. It contained a dangerous poison chemical, and thankfully it had a child-proof lid that Sam could not operate. If he had managed to get the bottle open and drink it, he could have become very ill. He might have even died. So, of course, Sam's dad said no and refused to open the bottle. He made the right decision.

In the Bible, God promises us that He will always hear and answer our prayers. But He doesn't always answer our prayers the way we want Him to. Sometimes God says yes, and we are thankful when He does. But at other times, God says no to us. It is not that He doesn't want to answer, for we know He loves all and wants His children in faith to pray. Jesus came to our world to save us from our sins, didn't He? Of course, He loves us. But God is not going to give something that is bad or that may cause harm. So sometimes He says no to prayers. Or He might say "not yet," or "something better" than what was asked for.

When we pray, Jesus tells us to say, "Let your will be done on earth as it is done in heaven" (Matthew 6:10). And those are difficult words to say! We want our own will to be done, and not God's. But that's the way God will answer our prayers. He will answer them according to His will and what is going to be the best for us. We need to remember this when Jesus says in the Bible, "If you ask the Father for anything in my name, he will give it to you" (John 16:23). God knows what is best for us, just like Sam's dad knew what was best for his son. God promises that He will answer all our prayers. But He will give only what is right, and He will give it just at the time it will do the most good.

God wants us to always talk to Him any time we want to. This is why we pray. In the Bible, St. Paul tells us, "Never stop praying. Whatever happens, give thanks, because it is God's will in Christ Jesus that you do this" (1 Thessalonians 5:17-18).

Remember, God loves to hear from us. And He will continue to answer our prayers in His own way, in His own time, and according to His divine knowledge, even if the answer is *no*.

REFLECTIONS: Has God ever said no to one of your prayers? Do you think that the all-knowing God may have more information about our needs than we do, especially during these uncertain times and interrupted seasons? Do you add to your prayers, "If it is your will, dear Lord?"

PRAYER: Heavenly Father, I thank you for saying yes to my many prayer requests. Also, thank you for saying no when it is the right thing to do. Give me patience when the answer is "not yet" or "something better." In Jesus' name, we pray. Amen

FOR FURTHER READING: Psalm 17:1-8.

21

God didn't give us a cowardly spirit but a spirit of power, love, and good judgment.

2 Timothy 1:7

PACKING UP

The family was sitting around the table. Father, Mother, and the three children were busy making lists. The fires in California had started early in that year, 2020, burning just a few miles away. The family was putting together their lists of things that each wanted to take when they were evacuated.

Dad reminded them, "We have the SUV and the pickup with the camper on it and a small trailer to haul behind. Think about the things that you would not be able to replace if they are lost." The eldest son spoke up and said, "Brownie, our dog, is going! She has been a member of our family for as long as I can remember." The girl said, "You will take all our old photo albums and scrapbooks, won't you, Mom?" "Yes," Mom replied, "and I'm packing the picture of Jesus and my collection of crosses too." The little boy spoke up (there wasn't anything on his list), "I don't feel good, Dad. I'm scared. Are we going to be all right?"

Dad thought this would be a perfect opportunity, as he reached for the Bible. He opened the book and said, "Sometimes God protects us in miraculous ways. 'He [God] will put his angels in charge of you to protect you in all your ways (Psalm 91:11).'" Mother added, "God expects us to trust Him. I think there is a place where the apostle Paul talked about that," as she looked to her husband. "I'll see if I can find it," he said as he paged to the back of the Bible. "Here is where he said it," and read from the Bible. He read about Paul trusting in God to care for him. "I know of whom I trust. I'm convinced that he is able to protect what he had entrusted to me until that day" (2 Timothy 1:12). "Another good verse is from Proverbs 3:5-6," Dad said, "'Trust the Lord with all your heart, and do not rely on your own understanding. In all your ways acknowledge him and he will make your paths smooth.'"

Dad said, "Don't you think it is interesting that Grandpa and Grandma moved into a great big house in Nevada with plenty of room to spare. What a blessing that we can come and stay with them." He continued, "So, God is directing our path, and we have someplace to go. We have a lot of work to do, packing and getting things ready. There is one more Scripture verse that we should keep in our hearts these next few days. It's from Psalm 34:7, I'll read it to you. 'The Messenger [angel] of the Lord camps around those who fear him, and he rescues them.' Now, let's pray the Lord's Prayer together."

REFLECTIONS: Are you afraid of storms? Can God protect us, even during a storm or a forest fire? Are disturbing things like storms or forest fires a surprise to God? Can you thank God even when it's difficult?

PRAYER: Dear Lord God. You know all things. You have an answer to everything because you know the end before the beginning. Please keep your protecting hand over us. No matter what happens, we trust you to be with us. Let your holy will be done in our lives and in our world. We ask it in Jesus' name. Amen.

FOR FURTHER READING: Psalm 91:1-10.

22

So if the Good News that we tell others is covered with a veil, it is hidden from those who are dying. The god of this world has blinded the minds of those who don't believe. As a result, they don't see the light of the Good News about Christ's glory. It is Christ who is God's image. Our message is not about ourselves. It is about Jesus Christ as the Lord.

2 Corinthians 4:3-5

CAN YOU SEE THE LIGHT?

The whole family had gathered to celebrate Mother's birthday. The three children, Mom, and Dad were all seated around the large round table in the dining room. They had just finished singing "Happy Birthday," and the mother had just blown out the candles.

All of a sudden, the lights went out. Everything was dark all over town. There had been a power failure due to the fires that were raging in the hills above. Father got up to find a flashlight but stubbed his toe. The youngest son tripped, and the baby cried.

Finally, Mother lit one of the candles again on the cake. Then at least everyone could see a little. It was a lot better than being in the dark. "Can you see the light?" Mom asked everyone.

You know there are a lot of people in the dark in another way. Many are lost in the darkness of their lives. In their darkness, they don't know which way to go. They stumble around in their lives, hurting themselves and others. If they could only learn of Jesus, they would see the light. Our Savior said of himself, "I am the light of the world. Whoever follows me will have a life filled with light and will never live in the dark" (John 8:12). When we know Jesus in faith, then we can see the way to God and the way of goodness. We can serve God and help others. Jesus assures us, "I am the way, the truth, and the life. No one goes to the Father except through me" (John 14:6).

It's like that family at the birthday party when the lights went out. In the darkness, none of them could see to do anything or to help each other. Only when the candle was lit could they see at all. In a similar way, once we have seen Jesus (the light of the world) in faith, then we can see the way to God. We are no longer in darkness.

Can you see the light of Jesus? If so, shine that wonderful Gospel light around so that others can see His light too! The apostle Paul tells believers, "Encourage each other and strengthen one another as you are doing" (1 Thessalonians 5:11). These uncertain times give us ample opportunity to help and encourage one another.

REFLECTIONS: Do you have a flashlight to help you see in the dark? Have you ever stumbled in the dark at night? Have you tried to show the light of Jesus to anyone who may be in the darkness of unbelief?

PRAYER: Help us show your light, Jesus, so others can find the way out of the darkness into the wonderful light of your love. Help us to share your light with others. Lead us in the way you want us to go. It is your name that we ask it. Amen.

FOR FURTHER READING: Psalm 119:105-110.

23

The message of the cross is nonsense to those who are being destroyed. But it is God's power to us who are being saved.

1 Corinthians 1:18

WHICH CROSS?

The neighborhood school was closed because of the virus. So Tally walked down the street to visit her cousin, Anna. They sat in the swing on the porch and visited. They were comparing their necklaces. One had a cross with Jesus on it. The other had an empty cross on her chain. "Why is your cross empty, and my cross has Jesus on it?" Anna asked. "I don't know," Tally answered, "Let's ask your Mom."

The girls went into the kitchen where Mom was working and sat at the table. They asked about the crosses. Mom answered, "There is a simple explanation," as she looked at their necklaces. "Would you like a glass of milk and some cookies?" she said. Mom sat next to them at the table with a cup of coffee and continued. "You should be proud to wear your necklaces. The cross with Jesus on it reminds us of how our Savior suffered for our sins. And because of what Jesus did, we are forgiven. This we believe with all our hearts!"

Mom went on, "But what does the empty cross remind us of? When you see a cross without Jesus hanging there, it reminds us that His suffering is now over. It was all done when

Jesus cried out on the cross, 'It is finished' (John 19:30). And after three days in the grave, He rose to life again. So the empty cross reminds us that the suffering of Jesus is finished and the that He has risen from the dead."

So both crosses are very meaningful for us. Best of all, they both remind us of Jesus and His great love for us. The cross is a great reminder for us of our wonderful Savior, Jesus. Oh, how we want to thank, praise, love, dedicate our lives to Him, and give our all to Him, who gave His all for us! Oh, how we remember the cross. We remember the empty tomb as well, Jesus. We will always love you for the love you have shown to us.

REFLECTIONS: Do you own a cross? Do you have a cross on the wall of your home? What do you think of when you see a cross?

PRAYER: Dear Jesus, the cross is a symbol of your love for us. You were willing to suffer even that terrible pain of the cross to pay for our sins and earn us a place in heaven. How can we thank you enough for your willing sacrifice of the cross for us? We say, "Thank you," and we honor and praise your name for your love. In your holy name, Jesus, we pray. Amen.

FOR FURTHER READING: Psalm 98:1-9.

24

Be filled with the Spirit by reciting psalms, hymns, and spiritual songs for your own good. Sing and make music to the Lord with your hearts. Always thank God the Father for everything in the name of our Lord Jesus Christ. Place yourselves under each other's authority out of respect for Christ.

Ephesians 5:18-21

THANK GOD FOR THE LITTLE THINGS

We usually remember to thank God for the big and important things He has done for us. Like sending Jesus to be our Savior from sin and earning us a place in heaven. Yes, Lord, we believe! In addition to the wonderful blessing of salvation through Jesus, there are other important things that God blesses us with. Like helping us avoid a serious illness like the COVID-19 virus, supporting Mom and Dad when their business is failing, or keeping us safe from a car accident or a house fire. God helps us with some really big things sometimes and does it in ways we could not, nor would expect. God says to us in Isaiah 55:8-9, "'My thoughts are not your thoughts, and my ways are not your ways,' declares the Lord. 'Just as the heavens are higher than the earth, so my ways are higher than your ways, and my thoughts are higher than your thoughts.'" Thank you, God!

But too often, we fail to thank our Lord for the many small blessings He showers upon us every day. For example, have you ever thanked God for the warm sunshine beaming through the window on a spring day? It is so nice to feel the warmth after a long, cold winter. How about the smell of flowers in the air, the good taste of an apple when you bite into it, fresh water to quench our thirst, or the beauty of a colorful sunset? When you are coughing with a cold, have you remembered to thank God for all those days of good health you have had in your life? What blessings can compare with a loving family—sharing and caring for one another? Compare this to other families where there are bitterness and arguments continually.

There are a lot of delicious, enjoyable, and comfortable things in our life that are small but truly important blessings. Yes, in the world, there is plenty of sin, problems, pain, and much more that Satan loves to heap upon us. But in spite of all that, there is still a lot of good that God sends our way. Our blessings may come in moments of crisis, or they may be the small things that He does for us every day. If it is good, it has come from God. The apostle Paul encourages, "Whatever happens, give thanks, because it is God's will in Christ Jesus that you do this" (1 Thessalonians 5:18). And in the Psalms, we read, "Give thanks to the Lord because he is good, because his mercy endures forever. Who can speak about all the mighty things the Lord has done? Who can announce all the things for which he is worthy of praise?" (Psalm 106:1-2).

REFLECTIONS: What are some really big things that you would want to thank God for? What are some very small things that you might want to thank God for? What time in the day or night do you remember to talk to God in prayer?

PRAYER: Dear heavenly Father, it is hard to find the right words to thank and praise you for all the blessings toward us, the big ones and the small ones. We simply say, "Thank you, God." In Jesus' name we pray. Amen.

FOR FURTHER READING: Psalm 92:1-9.

25

People should think of us as servants of Christ and managers who are entrusted with God's mysteries. Managers are required to be trustworthy.

1 Corinthians 4:1-2

COVID-19 TREE

Mom was sitting at the kitchen table when her little boy came through and filled a small pitcher with water. And out the back door he went. After he had filled the pitcher two more times, the mother became curious and waited to see where he was going. This time she followed him out the back of the house to the garden in the yard.

"What are you doing?" she asked her son. The boy answered, "I'm watering a baby tree." There in the garden stood a seedling of a small maple tree. It was about two feet tall, but you could tell it had been lovingly cared for.

"What made you decide to take care of a baby maple tree?" Mom asked. The boy replied, "So many bad things have happened this summer. People have gotten sick and died from the virus. Bad people have burned down buildings and have hurt people. And fires and storms have caused so much damage in so many places. So I planted a tree and am caring for it so I could show God that I was taking care of His world. He is so good to care for me and our family."

That's right, you know. God in His Word, the Bible, promises, "I will never abandon you or leave you" (Hebrews 13:5). He also made a promise long ago, "As long as the earth exists, planting and harvesting, cold and heat, summer and winter, day and night will never stop" (Genesis 8:22). These promises He keeps right now.

Wow! God takes care of us, even in these uncertain times and interrupted seasons. God is in control, even when things seem a bit out of control. We are encouraged to trust Him in Proverbs 3:5, "Trust the Lord with all your heart, and do not rely on your own understanding." What a great God He is! Every day we thank, praise, worship, and love Him. Maybe we will try harder to take care of His world even now, like planting or watering a baby maple tree.

REFLECTIONS: Are there ways that you can help take care of our planet? Do you pick up trash from the ground and put them in a garbage can? Do you thank God for the simple things, like fresh water, clean air, and warm sunsets?

PRAYER: Dear Lord God, there are too many things wrong in our world. It's not your fault, but the fault of sin in the world and in us. Still, you have provided many wonderful and great things in our world that are good and of great benefit to us. There are trees that give us fruits and nuts. The mountains are majestic, and the lakes are full of fish for us to eat. Help us to appreciate what good there is in life and to give it our care and concern. Continue to bless us, O Lord, even in these difficult and trying times. In Jesus' name, we ask it. Amen.

FOR FURTHER READING: Psalm 148:7-14.

26

Have the same attitude that Christ Jesus had. Although he was in the form of God and equal with God, he did not take advantage of this equality. Instead, he emptied himself by taking on the form of a servant, by becoming like other humans, by having a human appearance. He humbled himself by becoming obedient to the point of death, death on a cross.

Philippians 2:5-8

WHICH IS MORE IMPORTANT?

The increase of the virus infection had prompted the high school to return to distance learning again. So the two sisters were once more at home with Mom. It was November, and the girls watched as their mother put out the Christmas decorations in the front yard.

When Mom came back in, she heard her daughters arguing. Anne said, "I think Easter is most important!" Susan said even louder, "No, it isn't! Christmas is more important! Everyone has a Christmas tree, there are gifts, Mom makes especially good food, and even the stores and streets are decorated. And besides all that, it's Jesus' birthday! That's why Christmas is the most important church holiday." Annie would not give in, "All that is just extra and doesn't mean much. It is when Jesus died and rose again that we were saved. That's the most important thing ever!"

Mom was the peacekeeper and general referee in the family, and she thought it was time to step in. "There is no real right or wrong answer here," she said. "Both Christmas and Easter are very important in the church year. Almost all the world celebrates Christmas. We know that some people just get caught up in the spirit of the season, and they don't really understand the true meaning of the day. They will have a tree to decorate in their homes, they will exchange gifts, and they will get together with their families. But we who love Jesus in faith know the real meaning of Christmas. It's the time we remember the birthday of our Lord Jesus. That is the time when God became man to begin our salvation. It really is an important day for Christians!"

"But Easter is a special day for us too!" Mom continued. "The reason that Jesus came to our world as a man was to live perfectly in our place and to suffer and die on the cross to pay for our sins. That's the wonderful gospel message in Christ!"

Mom was right in her explanation. It's in the spring, during the Lenten season, we talk about when our Lord Jesus was on trial, when He was whipped and mocked, and when He died on the cross. And on Easter we celebrate His coming to life again. If we believe this, then when we die, we who love Him in faith will live again with Him in heaven. The Bible promises: "Everyone who believes in him [Jesus] will not die [perish] but will have eternal life" (John 3:16).

So both Anne and Susan were right about these special holidays. Christmas and Easter both deal with something important concerning Jesus. Christmas reminds us of His birth, and Easter reminds us of His death and His coming to life again. All of Jesus' life is special for us! Through faith in

Him, we have forgiveness of our wrongs and a promise from God of eternal life in heaven. On both Christmas and Easter, we want to honor and praise and thank our heavenly Father, for sending His Son, Jesus, into our world and into our lives.

The sisters seemed happy with their mom's explanation. Then Mom encouraged, "Now give each other a hug. I'm going to the kitchen," she added. "Who wants hot chocolate with marshmallows?"

REFLECTIONS: What decorations at Christmas point to Jesus? What does the empty tomb mean at Easter? In what special ways do you celebrate Christmas and Easter?

PRAYER: Thank you, Jesus, for Christmas. And thank you, Jesus, for Easter. Thank you for coming to our world and being our Savior. And thank you for your great love for us. We honor and praise your holy name. Amen

FOR FURTHER READING: Philippians 2:9-11.

27

Don't let evil conquer you, but conquer evil with good.

Romans 12:21

THEY DIDN'T DO A THING

We can get in trouble by *doing* a lot of things wrong, can't we? Like the two boys who finally returned to school after months of learning at home due to the virus, they didn't follow the rules. They didn't wear their masks and never stayed the proper distance from others. They got into a fight over who was going to be first in line. Billy received a black eye, Tom tore his shirt, and they both were sent to the principal's office by their teacher.

Sometimes, it's not what we *do* wrong but what we *say*. Another time Billy and Tom didn't start a fight, but they called each other bad names. They had to stay after school. Once they even got into trouble by thinking bad thoughts. Because they were looking mean and hateful at one another, the teacher made them take a time-out.

But do you know that we can do wrong by doing absolutely *nothing*. Let me tell you how that happens. The same two boys, Billy and Tom, were walking down the street when an elderly lady in front of them tripped and fell hard on the sidewalk. She dropped her grocery bag, and she hurt herself. Billy and

Tom walked by, pretending to ignore her. Now this time, those boys didn't do a thing—absolutely nothing. But, they *should have* done something to help, and because they *did not*, Billy and Tom were wrong. I hope none of us ever do as many bad things as those two boys did!

We know from God's Ten Commandments that we are to be kind and loving to one another. We are to look for ways to be caring and helpful. These uncertain times and the problems they have created give us ample opportunity to help one another. Not that we expect anything in return for our kindness. We simply are passing on the love we have received from God through our Lord Jesus Christ. In spite of our wrongs, Jesus gave His life for us on the cross. That is *true love*! We accept what He did in faith and truth.

Jesus said to us, and all believers, "Love each other as I have loved you. This is what I am commanding you to do" (John 15:12). With the help of God, we Christians try so very hard to be kind, generous, patient, and loving to others. And the apostle Paul wrote by inspiration of God, "I pray that your love will keep on growing because of your knowledge and insight. That way you will be able to determine what is best and be pure and blameless until the day of Christ," (Philippians 1:9-10). Because we love Jesus, we want to avoid doing anything wrong. With the help of Jesus, we want to do many things that are good for Him and helpful to others.

REFLECTIONS: Have you showed kindness to someone today? Do you look for ways to be helpful to others? Ask God to make you more aware of what help other people may need.

PRAYER: Dear Lord God, with your help, we can do all things. We do this not to gain your approval or a place in heaven. You have saved us by Jesus' life, death, and resurrection. But with your help and guidance and support, we can and want to love as you have loved us. In the name of Jesus, we pray. Amen.

FOR FURTHER READING: Psalm 34:12-22.

28

No one can tame the tongue. It is an uncontrollable evil filled with deadly poison. With our tongues we praise our Lord and Father. Yet with the same tongues we curse people, who were created in God's likeness. Praise and curses come from the same mouth. My brothers and sisters, this should not happen!

James 3:8-10

BUTTERED BREAD

The neighborhood bike repair shop was closed because of the COVID-19 virus. So Tommy, a nine-year-old boy, was working on his bike himself. The chain had come off, and he was trying to fix it but was having a hard time doing it. He kicked the bike and swore in frustration, "God curse this bike."

Grandma Julia was sitting on the porch nearby and heard him. "Tommy," she said, "don't say words like that!" "I know," he said, "but it is so hard to fix this bike, and I have tried for almost an hour." Grandma replied, "That is no excuse for asking God to curse the bike." "What do you mean?" he asked. "Well," Grandma said, "to curse something or someone is to ask for evil to come. If you have to say something in your anger, say 'buttered bread.' That way, God's name is not misused, nothing is cursed, and you can say it without harming anyone or displeasing God."

Tommy learned a good lesson that day from his grandma. What you say is important to the people around you. And it is important to God, too, especially if you use His holy name in anger. Remember God's commandment, "You shall not take the name of the Lord, your God, in vain." The catechism asks the question: "What is cursing by God's name?" And the answer is: "Cursing by God's name is speaking evil of God, or calling down evil from Him upon oneself, other persons, or any creature or thing." (Like cursing a bike.)

How should we use God's name? God would have us constantly use His name in prayer, praise, and thanksgiving. People are listening and watching Christians, children too, to see how they behave as followers of Jesus. Do they honor God and His holy name? Are they patient and kind and quick to help others in need?

What we as Christians do or say can be an encouragement to people who do not know Jesus as their Savior. Or, what we do or say can be a way for unbelievers to never want to know Jesus. The Bible also promises that "The gift that God freely gives is everlasting life" (Romans 6:23). So, knowing Jesus in faith is so very important for us and for everyone else too.

So, what Grandma Julia was saying to Tommy is that we should be careful with what we say. If you want to say something when things are not going well, say "buttered bread." That way God's name is not misused, no one is cursed, and no one is unhappy or turned away from Jesus.

REFLECTIONS: Am I careful with how I use God's name? Do I have a substitute word to say like "buttered bread"? Is God pleased by the way I talk?

PRAYER: Thank you, Jesus, for your love. We love you and want you to help us use your holy name in the way that will please you. And may, many, many more people learn to love you too. In your name, Jesus, we ask it. Amen.

FOR FURTHER READING: Psalm 19:8, 12-14.

29

No one else can save us. Indeed, we can be saved only by the power of the one named Jesus and not by any other person.

Acts 4:12

WHY?

Why, why, why? Many are asking this about the virus, the lockdowns, the riots, and unemployment today. This is a difficult time to endure and understand. But none of this is a surprise to God. He knows the problem before it happens. And He knows the answer to it all. We just trust Him to care for us, to protect us, and to provide for our needs. God has said that He will never leave us or forsake us, and this is found in Hebrews 13:5.

Many children ask the question "Why?" about many things. Like, "Why is the sky blue?" Or "Why is it cold in winter and hot in the summer?" Or "Why do dogs bark and cats meow?" Or "Why do we put butter on bread?" One very important "why-question" is about God. Children may ask, "Why is it important to know about Jesus?" One Bible passage will give the answer. It says in John 3:36, "Whoever believes in the Son has eternal life, but whoever rejects the Son will not see life. Instead, he will see God's constant anger." There are some big words here and some important lessons. "God's constant anger" means that God is really unhappy with those who do not love Jesus. And God will turn His back on them.

This is a very serious thing to happen. All people would like to be in heaven. The good news in this same Bible verse is that whoever believes in Jesus and loves Him will indeed be with Him in heaven. This comes at the end of a person's life. That may seem a long way off for children, but closer for those who are older.

Think about what it will be like in heaven. All believers will be with Jesus in a place where everything will be good. No virus, no bullets, no riots, no fires, and no hate; only wonderful years of eternity in God's comfort and joy. What a time it will be! And it will last forever and ever! Wow, thank you, Jesus, for earning a place for us in your heaven by your perfect life, lived for us, and by your death on the cross and resurrection. Thank you, Jesus! Thank you.

So, why is it important to know Jesus? Why, why, why? No love for Jesus—no heaven. When we love Jesus—we will always be with Him in heaven. Sounds great, doesn't it?

There are many things we don't understand. Not only do children wonder why, but so do many others. We all want to remember that God loves us. He is in control—He's got this!

REFLECTIONS: Are you sure you are going to heaven? Because of Jesus and your faith in Him, you indeed are going to heaven. Is Jesus fixed in your heart?

PRAYER: Jesus, I repent of my sins. I look to you for forgiveness. I want you to be a part of my life. I want to turn my life over to you. Lord Jesus, I believe. Blessed be your holy name. Amen.

FOR FURTHER READING: John 5:19-21.

30

This is eternal life: to know you, the only true God, and Jesus Christ, whom you sent.

John 17:3

ARE THEY RICH OR POOR?

A family was driving down the road one day in their old and very rusty van. All of a sudden, part of the back fender fell off onto the roadway. As they quickly pulled to the curb, one of the children jumped out and ran back to the spot where the rusty fender had landed. She dragged it off the road before any other car might run over it. The father opened the back, threw the piece of metal in, and they continued on their way.

They arrived home a few minutes later at a rather small house that needed some repairs and paint. The family each took a grocery bag into the house. It looked like the children were wearing hand-me-down clothing. After the groceries had been put away and a meal quickly prepared, the family sat down for Saturday lunch. Before anyone began eating, the father took out the family Bible and read some verses from the Book of John. They all joined in the Lord's Prayer and the table prayer. After the meal, the father said to the children, "Take time to study your memory work for Sunday school tomorrow."

Tell me about this family. Are they rich or poor? They drove an old van that was falling apart, they lived in a small house that needed paint, and they wore very plain clothing. But, they were rich in a very special way. They knew and loved the Lord Jesus. They were happy to hear His Word and to follow Him in their Christian lives. They knew the "one thing needful." They had the richest treasure of all, for they knew the Lord in faith. Christians "have peace with God because of what our Lord Jesus Christ has done," God assures us through the apostle Paul in Romans 5:1.

Jesus said at one time while talking about food, clothing, and such, "Be concerned about his [God's] kingdom and what has his approval. Then all these things will be provided for you" (Matthew 6:33).

Are you rich, or are you poor? No matter what you have in this life, if you know Jesus in faith as your Savior, you are truly rich indeed!

REFLECTIONS: How much "stuff" do you need to be happy? Are you content with the simple things? Have you thanked God today for helping you in your life?

PRAYER: Dear heavenly Father, we thank you for what you have given us in this life, the many blessings we enjoy every day. Even in these times of uncertainty, we are blessed with your constant love for us. Yet, our deepest thanks is for the Savior you have sent us. Without Jesus, we are lost. But with Him in hearts of faith, we have forgiveness and your promise of eternal life. "Whoever believes in the Son [Jesus] has eternal life" (John 3:36). Praise and honor to your holy name for these eternal riches we have received through your Son, Jesus Christ. In His name we pray. Amen.

FOR FURTHER READING: Psalm 106:1-4.

31

Never worry about anything. But in every situation let God know what you need in prayers and requests while giving thanks. Then God's peace, which goes beyond anything we can imagine, will guard your thoughts and emotions through Christ Jesus.

Philippians 4:6-7

WHAT IF?

A young girl and her father were talking one day. The daughter said, "What if I get the virus? What if the riots come to our town and things are burned down?" she cried. A lot of people are asking this in these uncertain times, "What if? What if?" "It's hard not to think about bad times in your life, isn't it?" the daughter said. Dad put his arms around her and gently hugged her. "Being positive is a choice you can make," he replied. "Remember what Mom often says. Many times you have heard her say, 'I can do all things through Christ who strengthens me.' Whatever is going on in your life, be sure to include God. Talk to Him in prayer because He loves to hear from you."

"Let me share something with you," her father said. He got out the family Bible and paged through to what he wanted to share with his daughter. He continued, "Listen to these encouraging words, 'Keep your thoughts on whatever is right or deserves praise: things that are true, honorable, fair, pure, acceptable, or commendable...Then God who gives his peace will be with you'" (Philippians 4:8-9). Dad concluded, "These are good words to think about and live by. They give encouragement and blessings to all who practice them."

These are indeed good words to follow and to practice in our lives, for all of us. Not only is it important because it comes from God's Word, the Bible, but it is so pleasant and encouraging to think about positive, hopeful things for the future, especially in these trying times of uncertainty and unrest. It's about your *attitude*. That is a big word, which has to do with how we think about things. God wants us to think about good things and to be hopeful in our lives. Remember, heaven waits for those who love and trust Jesus. The Bible promises, "Whoever believes in the Son [Jesus] has eternal life" (John 3:36). And God loves us right now, even while we are still in this world.

REFLECTIONS: Name three things you have worried about in the last few days. Were they as bad as you thought they might have been? Did you ask God for help?

PRAYER: Dear Jesus, help us to keep looking toward you and your love for us. We will be with you in heaven someday, but even now, you look after and bless us. There is no need to what if with you. You are the sure thing in our lives. Thank you, Jesus. Amen

FOR FURTHER READING: Psalm 112:1-8.

32

In this way you show that you are children of your Father in heaven. He makes the sun to rise on people whether they are good or evil. He lets the rain fall on them whether they are just or unjust.

Matthew 5:45

SIGNS OF GOD'S LOVE

Even though the effects of the pandemic have disturbed many things in our lives, there are still signs of God's love around us too. Take the seasons of the year. What is your favorite season? Some people love the snow and skiing of winter, while others look forward to the fresh green of spring and kite flying—still, others like the steamy hot days of summer and swimming or baseball. But many like the fall best of all. The fall has cool nights and pleasant days. The pumpkins are big and orange, the crops are ready to harvest, and there are no mosquitoes to pester you. It is a delightful time to be outside in the open air.

But best of all are the fall colors. The trees are turned into a splash of color, from red to yellow, brown, orange, and shades of green and gold. The beautiful colors just take your breath away. Of course, many children like playing in the fallen leaves. Raking them into big piles and then taking turns jumping into the middle. The leaves fly all around! Oh, the fall season is best of all!

Do you know that the changes which occur in the seasons are signs of God's love? The Lord made a promise long ago about the seasons of the year. In Genesis 8:22, God promised, "As long as the earth exists, planting and harvesting, cold and heat, summer and winter, day and night will never stop." God, in His love, has kept this promise all these years. Nighttime is always followed by daylight. Summer is always followed by fall, then winter, and spring. The seeds planted in the spring always bring a harvest in the fall. It always comes, as the Lord said it would. God has been faithful to His promises, in spite of all the evil in the world, such as riots, arson, stealing, hatred, and killings. But still, God sends the rain and the sun; night follows day, the winter is cold, and the summer is warm, as He promised.

Long ago, God also made another promise. He said He would send His Son to us. From the Bible, it says, "She [Mary] will give birth to a son, and you will name him Jesus [He saves]" (Matthew 1:21). When we turn to Jesus in love, then we are forgiven and saved. God's promises are always kept. They show His deep love for us.

Without the hand of God guiding and controlling things in the world, we would be in great trouble. What would happen if there was no summer? There would be no heat, no crops, and no food! What would have happened to us sinners had Jesus not come into the world?

But God is indeed faithful to His promises about the Savior, Jesus, just as He has been faithful about the changing seasons. For these wonderful promises, which are indeed signs of God's love for us, we thank and praise Him.

REFLECTIONS: What is your favorite season of the year? Do you see the hand of God controlling and guiding the things in this world? Can you rely on the promises of God?

PRAYER: Dear Lord Jesus, your promises are true and sure. We have full confidence in you and in your ability to help us. We bless and honor your name and offer you our thanks and praise. In your name, Jesus, we pray. Amen.

FOR FURTHER READING: Psalm 145:10-20.

33

God's saving kindness [grace] has appeared for the benefit of all people. It trains us to avoid ungodly lives filled with worldly desires so that we can live self-controlled, moral, and godly lives in this present world. At the same time we can expect what we hope for—the appearance of the glory of our great God and Savior, Jesus Christ. He gave himself for us to set us free from every sin and to cleanse us so that we can be his special people who are enthusiastic about doing good things.

Titus 2:11-14

TO MISS THE TARGET

The long summer days were giving way to the cooler days of autumn. Soon Dad would be bow hunting for deer. The extra meat would be a help for the family during these difficult times.

Dad was target practicing with his bow in the backyard. He was also taking time to help his twelve-year-old son to learn to pull the bow and shoot so he could hunt deer with him in the future. The boy snapped, "I missed again! Not only did I miss the bull's eye, but I missed the whole target!" He was getting very frustrated and was having a terrible time. "Don't be discouraged, Sam!" his father said in a reassuring voice. "It takes time to get used to the bow. And you need to build up your arm muscles a little bit. It will take some practice. "I'm getting tired," the son grumbled. "I'll never learn anything! I can't even hit the target. I'm a failure!"

Father figured it was time to change the subject and give his son a short rest. He asked, "Do you know that what we are doing reminds me of something in the Bible?" "Shooting an arrow has something to do with the Bible?" Sam asked, shaking his head. "Yes indeed," Dad continued. "One of the names for sin comes from shooting an arrow with a bow. I remember our pastor explaining it." He continued, "I don't remember what the Greek word for sin was, but I do recall what it meant. It meant to 'miss the mark or target,' like you have been doing this afternoon."

They both had sat down on the grass in the shade of the big oak tree in the backyard. Father continued intently, "we have a mark or target that we Christians try to hit with our lives. Because of our love for Jesus, we intend to follow the holy commands and will of God. Jesus himself said, 'You must be perfect as your Father in heaven is perfect' (Matthew 5:48). Perfection is our goal or target." "We really miss that goal, don't we?" Sam replied. "And we miss it often. God must get tired of our failures—of our sins."

Dad leaned back on the grass and stretched. "Yes and no," Father said seriously. "I'm sure God must get very impatient with us when we do wrong. But then, Jesus has already paid for our sins, and we are declared innocent. Those of us who repent of our sins and accept Jesus in faith are completely forgiven, and we shall be with our Savior forever in heaven. God promised it. Remember this verse? 'God loved the world this way: He gave his only Son [Jesus] so that everyone who believes in him will not die [perish] but will have eternal life'" (John 3:16).

"Now let's get back to hitting the target with our arrows!" Dad said. "We've rested long enough. Let's try to hit that old bull's eye again!"

REFLECTIONS: Have you missed any targets lately? Have you done something wrong that you shouldn't have? Have you tried to correct and improve something that you should be doing better? Did you ask God to help you?

PRAYER: Lord, teach us to hit the mark, to follow your commandments and will. When we miss, which too often we do, forgive us our errors and wrongs. We know you have promised to do that for us, for Jesus's sake. Amen.

FOR FURTHER READING: Psalm 86:1-3.

34

We know that all things work together for the good of those who love God—those whom he has called according to his plan.

Romans 8:28

HOMELESS

It had been several months since Dad's job had been closed down. Mom was working long hours at the nursing home. Money was tight, tempers were short, and the kids were feeling the tensions in the house. The virus and unrest seemed to go on and on,

Lori overheard her mom and dad talking about not being able to pay all the bills. They didn't sound very happy about it. "Are we going to be homeless?" she asked, frightened about what she heard. "Oh, no!" Dad said. "We are not going to be homeless. We have money in savings, and if we are careful how we spend, we will get through this pandemic."

"Everything is so scary right now," the little girl said. "We have to wear masks, we have to wash our hands often, we can't go to school, and we can't even play with our friends." Father hugged his little girl and said, "God will take care of us. I know this is a tough time, but mother and I know that God is watching over us and that He promises He will take care of us." Father sat down in his easy chair and reached for the family Bible, and opened it. "Jesus said in Matthew, 'Aren't two sparrows sold for a penny? Not one of them will fall to the ground without your Father's permission. Every hair on your head has been counted. Don't be afraid! You are worth more than many sparrows' (Matthew 10:29-31). God will see that we have clothes to wear, food to eat, and a place to live."

He turned the pages of the Bible and said, "We should try hard not to be afraid, but just trust God to love us. You know the sun will rise in the morning, the apples will ripen on the trees, the farmers will harvest the corn and wheat, and we will get through this pandemic. The Bible assures us, 'Even though I walk through the dark valley of death, because you are with me, I fear no harm. Your rod and your staff give me courage' (Psalm 23:4). Just like a shepherd takes care of his sheep, God takes care of all those who love Him. In future days and months, we will look back at this year, and it will be only a memory."

REFLECTIONS: Name three things that have opened and are back in business. Have you ever felt scared that you might become homeless? Have you asked God to take care of you during these bad times?

PRAYER: Thank you, God, for your love, your mercy, your comfort in tough times, your help in ways that we would not expect nor even imagine. Your ways are not our ways, and your thoughts are above our thoughts. You even promised us heaven when we love Jesus in faith. Take it on, God. Let your holy will be done. In Jesus' name, we pray. Amen.

FOR FURTHER READING: Psalm 106:1-6.

35

Everything has its own time, and there is a specific time for every activity under heaven...A time to plant and a time to pull out what was planted...a time to tear down and a time to build up, a time to cry and a time to laugh, a time to mourn and a time to dance.

Ecclesiastes 3:1-5

SEASONS

Did you receive your free calendar at the beginning of 2021? Usually, we get a number of calendars from a bank, an insurance company, a local store, or others. Sometimes, more calendars than we need or want. But this year, many have not received any calendars because the pandemic has slowed or interrupted a lot of things. How will we know what day, week, or month to plan things in our lives without a current calendar? A calendar marks the seasons of our lives.

God knows all about our days, past days, and days in our future. He knows all things and about all things in our lives. We are reminded of this in the Bible passage, Psalm 90:12, "Teach us to number each of our days so that we may grow in wisdom." Each day is a gift from God. What we do with our days is up to us. Do we waste our time daydreaming, napping, or doing nothing useful or helpful to us or anyone else? Or do we work and strive to live useful and productive days?

In Psalm 90, God reminds us, "Each of us lives for seventy years—or even eighty if we are in good health...Indeed, they are soon gone, and we fly away" (Psalm 90:10). And since each season of our lives is a gift from God, what should we do, how should we plan, and what would God like us to accomplish? How about starting each day with a prayer, thanking the Lord for another day, and asking Him what He would like us to get done this day. It would only take a few minutes to read a few Bible verses in the morning before breakfast. Share the verses with the family. Then we would be ready for the rest of the day.

When one gets older and looks back at the season of one's life, the days past have gone too fast. We remember things that have happened ten years ago, twenty years ago, and even longer. We remember past birthdays, past things we enjoyed, and some things that made us sad. We are never perfect, no matter what our age is. That is why we need our Lord Jesus. He was perfect in our place. He suffered on the cross to pay for the wrong things we did in the past, or maybe just today. There is a Bible passage that reminds us, in 2 Corinthians 5:15, "He [Christ] died for all people so that those who live should no longer live for themselves, but for the man who died and was brought back to life for them."

Let's not let the interruptions and uncertainties that have disturbed the seasons of our life stand in the way of our love for the Savior and for the work that He would have us do in His name.

REFLECTIONS: What have I done for Jesus today? What will I plan to do for Jesus tomorrow? Who can I help in a kind and caring way?

PRAYER: Dear Lord Jesus, show me what to do for you in the seasons of my life. Teach me to number my days right so that I may gain a heart of wisdom. Teach me to live not just for myself, but for you who lived, died, and rose again just for me. In your name, Jesus, I pray. Amen.

FOR FURTHER READING: Psalm 1:1-6.

36

If we are his children, we are also God's heirs. If we share in Christ's suffering in order to share his glory, we are heirs together with him. I consider our present sufferings insignificant compared to the glory that will soon be revealed to us.

Romans 8:17-18

THE CARD

She sat at the kitchen table with address book and sympathy cards scattered in front of her. It had been a long day sending out the bereavement cards of her husband, Jim. They had been married fifty-five years. A slip on the ice sent him to the nursing home for rehab. Marge, his wife, visited him daily until the home was locked down due to the COVID-19 virus. Marge often thought of the quick kiss and hug, the "I love you. God bless. I'll see you tomorrow." Those were the last words between her and her husband, Jim.

She was awakened out of her thoughts just then as the phone beside her rang. "Hello," she answered. It was her neighbor from three doors down. "How is it going?" she asked. "I can't imagine how you must be coping. It must have been so hard not being with Jim those last weeks. You never had a chance to see him again. Not to have a funeral to say your final goodbyes must have been heartbreaking."

Marge was quiet for a while as she looked through the sympathy cards on the table. When she found what she was looking for, she replied. "Jim had a very strong faith in Jesus as his Lord and Savior. We believed in the love and the salvation Jesus won for us. His death and resurrection gained a place in heaven for all who believe in Him. Jim believed that, and I know he is with Jesus in heaven right now. I got a card in the mail, and I love the comforting words it gives. I read it often, and I will share the words with you." Marge continued, "On the outside of the card, it reads, 'May God's promise bring you comfort…For believers death is not an end, but a beginning—a starting point that leads to everlasting life.' On the inside, there is a Scripture passage. It reads, 'God encourages us through St. Paul concerning our life in heaven, "I consider our present sufferings insignificant compared to the glory that will soon be revealed to us"'" (Romans 8:18). Marge went on to say, "On the opposite side it reads, 'A prayer for you…May God give you comfort in knowing that your loved one is home now, safe in the loving arms of our Savior.'"

The neighbor replied, "What nice sentiments those words are! I hope they give you lots of comfort. God bless you, Marge. I'll call again." Marge hung up. She sat there alone at the kitchen table with all the sympathy cards scattered before her. She picked up the card that she had just read, held it to her heart, bowed her head, and cried. Softly she prayed, "Thank you, Jesus. Take care of my Jim. I'll see him tomorrow, someday."

REFLECTIONS: Have you called someone to extend sympathy for the loss of a loved one? Send them a note—use the words from *The Card* devotion. Pray for God's comfort to all those who have suffered a loss.

PRAYER: Dear Lord, be with us day by day, in sickness or health, in life or death. You are truly the one who understands and is always there to comfort and support us. Help us to bring comfort and hope to those who are in need of it. In Jesus' name, we pray.

FOR FURTHER READING: Psalm 116:1-7.

37

We know that the Son of God has come and has given us understanding so that we know the real God. We are in the one who is real, his Son Jesus Christ. This Jesus Christ is the real God and eternal life.

1 John 5:20

HE NEVER CHANGES

"Am I supposed to wear a mask or not?" little Ann said. "Can I play with my friend, Julie, or not?" "Can I go to school, or do I have to stay at home?" Ann was questioning her parents. These times have been confusing, with the experts giving conflicting answers. Things keep changing rather fast in these uncertain times.

Is there anything certain and unchangeable that we can rely on? Good question! There is an answer—His name is Jesus! The Bible assures us, "Jesus Christ is the same yesterday, today, and forever" (Hebrews 13:8). He always was God, and He always will be God. He said of himself one time, "I am the way and the truth and the life. No one goes to the Father [God the Father] except through me" (John 14:6). Well, that sounds very solid and certain, doesn't it? With life so uncertain and changeable, it is nice to know the Lord Jesus, who never, ever changes. He always loves us, He is always our Savior from sin, and He has already prepared a place for us in heaven—for all who love Him in faith. That same chapter of John 14 records Jesus' words. He promised, "Believe in God, and believe in me. My father's house has many rooms. If that were not true, would I have told you that I'm going to prepare a place for you? If I go to prepare a place for you, I will come again. Then I will bring you into my presence so that you will be where I am" (John 14:1-3). That is a rock-solid promise made by Jesus himself.

How do we know His words are true and certain? We know it is true because all the Bible was inspired and guided to be written at God's command and guidance. The reading from 2 Timothy 3:16 says, "Every Scripture passage is inspired by God. All of them are useful for teaching, pointing out errors, correcting people, and training them for a life that has God's approval." And Jesus Himself said, as recorded in John 8:31-32, "If you live by what I say, you are truly my disciples. You will know the truth, and the truth will set you free." This is so comforting to know and believe. Jesus is the sure thing! He is going to get us through anything in this uncertain and changeable world—this old world of sin. Believe Him, love Him, trust Him, and look forward to a forever life with Him in a place that He has prepared just for you.

REFLECTIONS: Can you name something that has been a major change in your life? Can you name something that is getting back to normal? Can you name something that has not changed?

PRAYER: We thank you, Lord, every day, many times a day. We talk to you in prayer. We know you love to hear from us. We can pray, "Thank you, Jesus, for being such an important, steady part of our life. In your blessed name we pray. Amen."

FOR FURTHER READING: Psalm 73:25-26.

38

Always be ready to defend your confidence in God when anyone asks you. However, make your defense with gentleness and respect.

1 Peter 3:15

ANSWER

It was eight months and three weeks to the day since the old woman had been out of the house. The COVID-19 virus had kept her sequestered for all those months. MS had put her in a wheelchair, and other ailments made her very vulnerable to the virus.

"After our wellness checks at the doctor, I'll take you anywhere you want to go," her husband said. They had been married for fifty-three years. Her husband pushed her along in the wheelchair wherever they went. He was eighty-two, and she a few years younger. "Well, it is not Sunday, but my first choice would have been to attend church," she said. "Yes, that would be nice," he replied. She continued, "So, let's go to the mall. We will wear our masks and avoid the crowds."

Later on, that afternoon, as they were walking through the mall, a little boy approached them and asked, "Is it fun to ride in a wheelchair?" He was just curious since he had never seen someone in a wheelchair before. His mother caught up and scolded him, "Leave the woman alone and don't bother her." The woman in the wheelchair said, "It's all right for him to ask. How else will he learn?" She continued by saying, "It would be fun to ride in a chair like this if I didn't have to use it. I got sick, and the illness took away my ability to walk or to use my arms." "Are you scared?" the three-year-old boy asked. "No, I'm not scared." She nodded towards her husband and, smiling, said, "This guy takes care of me. And I know that God watches over me too."

Her husband added, "Our heavenly Father says, 'I will never abandon you or leave you'" (Hebrews 13:5). The old man continued to talk to the boy about Jesus and His great love for us all. He quoted the famous John 3:16, "God loved the world this way. He gave his only Son so that everyone who believes in him will not die [perish] but will have eternal life." The mother stood quietly, listening. She called her son, held his hand to leave. Then she turned back to the couple and said, "Thanks. I needed that!"

The apostle Peter encourages us, "Dedicate your lives to Christ as Lord. Always be ready to defend your confidence in God when anyone asks you to explain it" (1 Peter 3:15).

REFLECTIONS: Have you ever told anyone about Jesus? Has anyone ever asked you about Jesus? Can you think of some things you might say?

PRAYER: Help us, Lord Jesus, to love you in faith and to share our love for you with others. May the Holy Spirit give us the words to say and the confidence to say them. It is for your sake we ask this, Jesus. Amen.

FOR FURTHER READING: Psalm 34:1-4.

39

Be ready to spread the word whether or not the time is right. [In season or out of season] Point out errors, warn people, and encourage them. Be very patient when you teach. A time will come when people will not listen to accurate teachings. Instead, they will follow their own desires and surround themselves with teachers who tell them what they want to hear. People will refuse to listen to the truth and turn to myths. But you must keep a clear head in everything. Endure suffering. Do the work of a missionary. Devote yourself completely to your work.

2 Timothy 4:2-5

NON-ESSENTIAL CHURCH

When the COVID-19 virus arrived from China in the early spring of 2020, people had no idea the devastating impact it would have on our lives. The President closed our borders first to China and then to other countries. Travel was restricted even between states. Airplanes, trains, and other means of transportation were severely curtailed. The "new normal" started cropping up. Wearing masks, elbow bumps, and social distancing were expected. Great debates and arguments were had on what were essential activities and businesses and what were non-essential. All these pandemic rules and regulations varied from state to state. A person could go to the gym in one state but not in another. Some elementary schools might have full attendance, but not in another district.

Obeying the mandates and temporary rules and restrictions were now pronounced for the good of the community and country. When churches in some states were included with movie theaters and restaurants as non-essential, many Christians were upset. The former President stated that churches were essential.

Now Christians have to abide by the new normal in how to worship. Pastors take their church services on-line, to radio, and to TV stations. Churches that were closed to indoor worship have brought the service to their parking lot or on the lawn next to their church. But if you could worship in the church building, the number of members allowed is limited and social distancing in the pews is required.

Having difficulties in worshipping is not new. The early Christians had to worship in secret, as is the case in some countries today. Even though it has been difficult for Christians, the love that believers have for Christ has been the driving factor in bringing them together to worship.

Reverence for worship was God's commanded way back when he gave the Ten Commandments. He said, "You shall keep the day of rest holy." The Bible says, "We should not stop gathering together with other believers, as some of you are doing. Instead, we must continue to encourage each other even more as we see the day of the Lord coming" (Hebrews 10:25).

For many Christians, it is called the "Lord's Day," the day we honor God in our church. That makes Sunday a very special day for all who love Jesus in faith. He died and rose again to pay for our sins, and He has earned eternal life in heaven for us.

In church, we have the opportunity to encourage one another, listen to each other's problems, and pray for one another. We can raise our voices in prayer, praise, and thanksgiving, which is good and acceptable to God. "I was glad when they said to me, 'Let's go to the house of the Lord'" (Psalm 122:1).

Yes, the pandemic has changed the lives of many families. But let's not let it diminish or discourage us from going back to the most important activity in a Christian's life. That is attending church services with our loved ones and family at our side.

REFLECTIONS: Name the different ways you have been hearing God's Word. How many different ways have you been worshipping? What do you miss by not attending church?

PRAYER: Lord, protect our opportunities to join others in prayer and worship. We gain much support for our faith and encouragement in our lives from one another. We draw our strength from you, O God. We ask this in Jesus' name. Amen.

FOR FURTHER READING: Psalm 31:1-5.

40

Every good present and perfect gift comes from above, from the Father who made the sun and moon and stars. The Father doesn't change like the shifting shadows produced by the sun and the moon. God decided to give us life through the word of truth to make us his most important creatures. Remember this, my dear brothers and sisters: Everyone should be quick to listen, slow to speak, and should not get angry easily.

James 1:17-19

SCRAPBOOK

"Put that back," Mom said. Her daughter had pulled out an old worn face mask from the garbage can. "We don't keep those anymore," her mother scolded. "I'm making a scrapbook," her daughter replied, "of all the things about the virus and what happened during the pandemic. I thought it would be fun, but it seems to be a very unhappy scrapbook." Her mother said, "Yes, I know. You can become very depressed if you think about the things that happened last summer."

Mom continued, "I try to think about the positive things and the good times that we had together. We baked a lot that summer, and our garden and flower beds were big and beautiful. We gathered a lot of vegetables that we put away in the freezer. We would never have been able to do that if we did not have to stay home. And Dad took us fishing a lot. We all had a good time when we were fishing together!"

There are some words from the Bible that encourage us to think about things in a good way. "Finally, brothers and sisters, keep your thoughts on whatever is right or deserves praise: things that are true, honorable, fair, pure, acceptable, or commendable" (Philippians 4:8).

The apostle Paul encourages us in that same chapter, "Never worry about anything. But in every situation, let God know what you need in prayers and requests while giving thanks. Then God's peace, which goes beyond anything we can imagine, will guard your thoughts and emotions through Christ Jesus" (Philippians 4:6, 7). God also promises us, "I will never abandon you or leave you" (Hebrews 13:5).

The daughter grabbed the scrapbook and headed out of the kitchen. "Where are you going?" Mom asked. "I think I am going to look at this again and write about the good times we had together last summer. When I look back at the year, I will remember how God cared for us and how we took care of each other."

It's called *attitude*. How do we look at things, how do we remember events and happenings, or how do we look ahead to tomorrow? It is up to us. And with God's help and guidance, we can see His hand in everything we do, or say, or in whatever happens to us.

REFLECTIONS: Can you think of three or four things that you would put in your scrapbook? Can you think of three or four things you would not want to put in your scrapbook? It is good to thank God for the good things. Is there something in the bad that you can be thankful for?

PRAYER: Thank you, God, for your love and mercy and many blessings. If we made a list of all the good things you have given us, it would be a very long list. But we can be assured that the best is yet to come from you. Thank you, in Jesus' name. Amen.

FOR FURTHER READING: Psalm 143:8-11.

AFTERWORD

Years ago, when our daughter, Janna, was a little girl, she would ask, "Are we there yet? Are we there yet?" We would be on our way to the Weinhold farm. My wife, Sandy, would turn to the back seat and patiently say, "No, not yet, Honey. There are three curves, two farms, a stop sign, a long straight road, a mailbox, and up the hill to Grandpa and Grandma's." Our daughter knew when we turned off the highway onto the country road that we were getting closer and closer to the home place.

The pandemic, the weather events, the fires, the riots, and the deaths have many people wondering, "Are we there yet? Are these the end times? Are we getting close to our heavenly home place?" I don't have the answer. No one does. The answer to "Are we there yet?" is known only to God.

But *The Unstoppable Grace of God* has given me much encouragement. I would like to share one last and final Scripture in *Interrupted Seasons*. Our heavenly Father promises, "Don't be afraid, because I am with you. Don't be intimidated; I am your God. I will strengthen you. I will help you. I will support you with my victorious right hand" (Isaiah 41:10).

Take heart, dear friend. God has our back!

—Dave

ABOUT THE AUTHOR

David Jewett Nelson was born and raised in Lake Mills, IA. He attended Drake University in Des Moines. After feeling called to the ministry, he attended Bethany Lutheran Theological Seminary in Mankato, MN. He was ordained in 1970. Pastor Nelson served congregations of the Evangelical Lutheran Synod in Northern Minnesota, Portage and Wisconsin Dells, WI, Princeton, MN, and Mayville, ND.

After retiring from the full-time ministry, he joined the Lutheran Church Missouri Synod and served as visitation pastor at Holy Cross and Redeemer Lutheran Churches, St. Cloud, MN. Now completely retired, he lives with his wife of fifty-four years, Sandra, in St. Cloud. The Nelsons have one adult married daughter, Janna.

CPSIA information can be obtained
at www.ICGtesting.com
Printed in the USA
JSHW021508010521
14202JS00006B/114